Raising An Emotionally Charged Ostrich

Surviving Autism & ADHD with Honesty, Humour, & Low Standards

Rebel Jones

Published By *Rogue Words on Toast*

Rogue Words on Toast

ISBN: 978-1-0682120-0-0

Published by *Rogue Words on Toast*

Cover design and images by the Author
Printed in the United Kingdom
First edition: 2025

This book is for my beautiful family,
for surviving the chaos, the rants, the rewrites,
and the questionable parenting decisions.

To my son, who gave me the fire to write it all down.
To my daughter, who laughed both with me and at me,
and somehow made me believe I could actually pull this off.

To the parents juggling meltdowns, medical forms,
and microwave coffee - you're not alone.
You're doing better than it feels.

And to anyone out there winging it, faking it,
or holding it together with sarcasm and snacks…

This one's yours too.

Disclaimer

This book contains **adult content**, **potentially offensive language**, and **humour** that some may find **uncomfortable**. If you're easily offended or prefer a more *sanitised* experience, this might not be the book for you.

Expect references to offbeat topics, including my *beef with vegans, schools (specifically the frustrations of the traditional system), stereotyping, religion, drugs and hookers.* These are all made with the tongue in cheek - **absolutely zero malice here** - but please be aware that, as an '80s child and Millennial, I have a tendency to poke fun at the world around me. And if you're easily triggered by today's social sensitivities, you may want to proceed with caution.

If, however, you're ready for **unfiltered truths**, **chaotic parenting moments**, and a good laugh *(even at the messiest parts of life),* then buckle up and dive in.

I'm not here to sugarcoat or hold back - this is the real, raw, and occasionally irreverent journey through the world of neurodiversity, parenting chaos, and everything in between.

You're welcome.

You picked this book up thinking, or maybe hoping, it was a *'self-help'* guide to navigating neurodiversity. And technically, it is. Sort of.

But more than that, it's my story.

A somewhat unhinged, self-reflective, punch-you-in-the-nose-with-a-rubber-ducky kind of story. It's a tale of salami, drugs, and 80s rock music... Because, according to my eight-year-old son - the hero behind much of this chaos - it was *the* golden era for music. And I have to agree.

He is a musical genius in the making, as well as being autistic, having ADHD, and a way with words that will either comfort you in your darkest hour... Or lead you to psychoanalyse your most recent life choice... Depending on his mood.

He is more creative, clever, and stubborn than most adults I know. *(Yes, he gets the stubborn part from me. Don't judge!)* And living with him is like having a front-row seat to a recently-released-from-jail pyromaniac's show, with equal parts of amazement, fear, and utter unpredictability.

Some days, his mind is a spin cycle of ideas and questions that would stump a Hotpoint technician *(and his piano teacher, it would seem!)* And on other days, life feels like an Olympic event, where I'm the under-trained athlete trying to keep up with his relentless energy.

He's taught me more about neurodiversity than any expert ever could, simply by being himself. And he inspired me to follow my dreams and write. I mean, I've written for a long time - I was first published at thirteen with a poem entitled *'Life'... Oh, sweet naïve child, you had no idea!*

But without his and my almost teenage daughter's acceptance of who I am, of the love and courage they both show on a daily basis, I would not be doing this. I would not be taking this leap of faith... *Ok, it may be more reckless life movement with a can of Fanta, but we'll go with it*

Yes, my daughter is the calm in the storm, except when she *is* the storm. And while my son may be the fireworks display, she's the steady lighthouse in the distance...That is, until she's huffing and rolling her eyes with a precision only tweenagers can.

Honestly, she keeps me grounded, humbles me regularly, and reminds me that no matter how many tattoos I have, fast cars I drive, or baked goods I provide for drama club... I'm still not cool.

But I'm OK with that, just like I'm OK with my excessive drinking habit *(it's coffee!)* and I'm OK with having an emotional support team of cats. FYI, they're weirdly comforting and yet judgmental enough to keep me in check.

Now, a quick warning - if the watershed still existed, this book would not be appropriate to open beforehand. But since everything's on demand these days, I'm not responsible for your reading-time choices.

If you choose to dive into this, with kids over your shoulder or while sipping tea with Great-Aunt Mildred, that's on you. Hold onto that conscience, and rattle it like it owes you an apology for everything you've ever Googled at 2am.

And since we're on the topic of choices:

- For the standard experience, read the standard font. That's in Arial, because that's, well, standard.
- For the full effect, chaotic brain spirals and all, include the scribbled notes.
- And for a quiet life? Put the book down and go smell the flowers. I won't be offended... *Well, maybe a little. But I'll cry into a gluten-free croissant and get over it!*

I will, without question, throw in a barrage of unnecessarily big and complicated analogies, for no reason other than I like to. It's cheaper than therapy, and somehow makes the chaos feel like it has layers. Like a double-stack sandwich. Or a trifle. Or a really dysfunctional lasagne.

I will also, at some point, almost certainly offend the easily offendable. Not because I mean to, well, maybe a *little* bit, but more because I have the tact of a half-drunk aunt at a wedding, who's been left unsupervised near the microphone… and is now giving a heartfelt toast that somehow includes both a dead hamster and an accidental slip of the nip.

You've been officially warned *(just in case you missed the whole disclaimer at the front of the book!)*

Oh, and before I forget, for you parents and carers of kids on the spectrum, I'm going to share a few things that work for us. I can't promise they'll do the same for you, but maybe they're worth trying. Or tweaking. Or twerking along to. I don't know anymore…

And with that, I'd like to formally invite you into my wonderfully messy chaos, and the majillion and one beautiful bits that come with living in a neurodiverse house…

(It was either this or try my hand at writing children's stories. But apparently, my 'unique charm' isn't suitable for the under-5s crowd!)

Let's begin.

Chapter 1: Survival

For when 'getting through the day' is the only thing on the to-do list.

They say mornings are the most productive time of day. And if by *'productive'* you mean the best time to flick the kettle on and pretend the rest of the world doesn't exist, then yes, I'm absolutely nailing it.

My son? Not so much. He's more of a "*Mum, Mum... Mum, Muuuuum... Mum, Mum...*" at precisely 07:56 kind of person. This warm-up show is inevitably followed by, *"I need help with my pull-ups,"* or, if the universe really wants to set my world on fire, an enthusiastic open mic about his current obsessions or latest gameplay.

Honestly, there isn't enough coffee in the pot to deal with either of these situations at that hour of the day. Scratch that - there isn't enough coffee on the entire planet!

Now, don't get me wrong. My son is brilliant. He's hilarious, outgoing, and full of charm, not least of all with his *"Ladies first"* at every shop doorway. But mornings? Mornings with him are a *special* kind of challenge.

While I'm stood clutching my coffee mug like it contains the secret to a perfect Yorkshire pudding, he'll be there, ricocheting around with the energy of someone who's already had three espressos and a packet of Skittles. It's like living with a 4ft whirlwind who communicates mostly in questions, sudden movement, and inexplicable grunting.

Oh, and then there's Norah. Norah's a cat, our cat. But in her mind, she's the CEO of the household. She'll perch on the bathroom cabinet, staring at me with contempt, as if to say, *"Is this really the best you can do? Look at your hair. Look at your life."*

Yeah, thanks, Norah. I already know, OK.

Frankie, on the other hand, Frankie, Frankenstein, The Frankster, is a typical orange-flavoured feline. There's not a whole lot going on between his big, goofy ears. He just bounces between the rooms like a ping-pong ball. And let it be known when he's hungry or needs attention. But honestly? I kind of respect that.

Because at the end of the day, we've all got to do what we've got to do. We make it work, just to survive. And really, that's what this chapter is all about. *Survival.*

Full disclosure... Some days, it feels like that's all I'm doing - just getting through the day, with nothing to spare.

Yes, the house, at times, looks like a crime scene, complete with dubious marks on the walls. My clothes, a tragic mash-up of *'Aging without dignity'*, and many a bad fashion and/or life choice.

And my Amazon deliveries remain on the doorstep, practically stamped with a '*Take Me'* sign for the local looter. Because even the thought of answering the door feels like too much to ask.

But here's the thing - after many late-night, *"Why am I the world's crappiest parent?"* pity parties, I've realized those days are part of the package. And you know what? They're totally OK.

As I edit this, my son is singing 'Halle-monia' (because he can't say 'Hallelujah') mixed with spooky sounds, varying pitches of 'meow', and 'frog' hiccups in the background... Just to keep things real! He's got this robot that mimics his crazy repertoire, and the current 'conversation' between them is hysterical, if but a wee bit distracting!

It's not always like that - a bare bones survival gig. For the most, I actually have things semi-together... Well, compared to the days that I don't.

As a *so-obviously-but-not-yet-diagnosed-ADHDer* myself, the chaos can be hard to control. The days are long, but often full of procrastination. And the nights are spent trying to catch my breath in a pool of worry and uncertainty.

Not gonna lie, or dress it up in pretty bows - raising kids is tough. Raising kids with additional needs, even more so.

Tougher than swallowing your Grandma's *'special soup'*, with a heavy dose of *'I have no idea what's going on'* mixed through. Tougher than the hallway bullying of high school - urgh, those years nearly broke me *(especially when we moved from England to Edinburgh. And as the only 'posh' kid in a rough city school... well, you can imagine!)*

And tougher still, than admitting that your parents, or grandparents in my case, were right when they said you'd screw up the first seventeen opportunities life throws at you... Which, for the record, I did, most spectacularly.

Honestly, if someone had told me twenty years ago that I'd be the go-to person for pull-up changes and chew toy finding, I'd have laughed, slowly backed away, and then bolted as if my life depended on it. I would've told them, straight up, that I'm not cut out for that kind of responsibility; that I'm nowhere near mentally equipped to care for someone whose needs seemingly discount the years they've lived, and unfairly replace them with a much younger, and less capable mindset.

But I was wrong, for it turned out that I am the ultimate teeth brusher, sock sorter, food encourager, Makaton user, and hyper-aware being in this house, with *oodles* and *noodles* and *squoodles* of love for my son and his older sister.

Besides, my boy isn't less capable. His talents just lie elsewhere. Piano playing seems to far exceed the need to toilet train, or put a hoodie on without getting stuck halfway in. And his long-term memory? Razor-sharp. He'll call you out on something you mumbled six months ago, word for word. Trust me - I've been held accountable more times than a dodgy politician, whether I made a promise, hinted at one, or merely sighed in a way that suggested agreement.

And truthfully? I admire it. He knows exactly what he wants and doesn't let the world make him forget it. He's completely cracked the code for living his best life, with *Queen* rocking it out in the background, and a large helping of purple fruit pouches on the side.

His worries extend no further than if his tablet battery life will make it to the end of the day. And he can find happiness in the simplest of things, be it finishing a really big book, eating ice cream on the beach in January, or having Mummy time whilst doing the weekly food shop.

Because for him, happiness isn't something to chase.

It's something he carries with him every single day. Whilst I'm rushing out the door, patting down pockets for my keys and phone, he's singing, or humming, or tapping away to his own rhythm.

He's not lost in the moment, but embracing it, like a tiny rockstar on a UK tour, completely unbothered by the chaos around him, while his roadie *(me)* scrambles to keep it all together.

I kind of imagine it like those silent discos, where everyone who's wearing headphones can hear the music pulse through their body. And the cares of life are left outside, muffled, distant, and just unimportant. Only my kid doesn't need the headphones. He's already in that beautiful place *(as frustrating as that can be when I'm trying to do something!)* And I am the one left on the outside, as the world hums with chaos.

I wish I had his ability, gift, or whatever you want to call it, to switch off from humanity and the tension it brings. He *is* so carefree, so unburdened with life that he can enjoy the moments that most of us, me included, let slip away.

Maybe it's because he has autism and ADHD, which naturally alter his view of the world, and allow him to filter out the noise. Or maybe it's because he's eight, and home educated, and allowed the freedom to be a child. I know for many neurodiverse children who are in school *(and just to be clear, I'm not saying school is bad - it's the right choice for plenty of kids),* the pressure to mask or '*fit in*' can be completely overwhelming.

It's like being told you need to shrink, just to make other people feel comfortable. To hold back parts of who you are because they don't match the room you're in. To drip-feed your personality in tiny, careful doses, like a tap that's only just holding it together.

And all while being expected to focus on 90-minute lectures about meter readings or beige ceiling tiles. Or... whatever brand of boring is being served that day. Take your pick.

I know, to an extent, that's life. I know we all have to *'tone it down'* for work, for social expectations. We learn to sand our edges, to fit into spaces that were never made for us. But if our children are *'sanded'* too early *(insert some weird mental image here… Child hoisted from the womb, skipping skin-to-skin contact and going straight in for a 60-grit rub down, followed by a 220 all over…),* then how will they ever know where they were meant to fit?

I know, I know - that sounds contradictory. One minute, I'm saying kids should be free to find where they belong. The next, they shouldn't be forced to fit in. All in a world that demands everyone fits *somewhere* but conveniently forgets that not everyone actually *does*… But what I actually mean is, there's a *'place'* for everyone, and they deserve the chance to walk their own yellow brick road to find it.

That being said, society sucks ba… No, I'm kidding…well, mostly.

I've met some really nice society toe-dippers. The type who are happy to perch on the edge of the pool, feet dangling just enough to feel accepted, without stripping naked and baring all... Metaphorically, of course!

But I've also met far too many self-important people. The type who believes that *'training your child'* to fall in line is essential. And anything less is considered child abuse.

"How else will they survive?" they ask, again and again, like a broken record of unsolicited parenting advice.

But as someone who actively avoids opening the front door to retrieve yet another Amazon haul *(seriously, I need a better drop-off point*), I can confirm that simply surviving isn't all it's cracked up to be. And forcing a child to *toughen up* certainly isn't the kind of *'encouragement'* I want my children to feel.

This isn't Boot Camp, ladies and gentlemen. And it's certainly not the

Victorian era, where children were expected to be seen and not heard. Oh no! My son, for one, is *very* good at being heard.

In fact, the term *"stampede of wildebeests"* comes to mind. As does *"Hummingbird crossed with a Screaming Piha",* which, in case you're wondering, is an exotic bird with a voice loud enough to haunt your dreams.

And honestly? That's exactly how it should be. Because life isn't about just keeping your head down and making it through the day. It's about finding joy, taking up space, and, if you feel inclined to do so, shouting about it along the way.

Random interjection (you'll find plenty of those in this book), but just this evening, as we parked up and emptied the car, I suddenly shouted loudly and with great theatrical flair (much to my daughter's embarrassment), that she's meeting her friend on Sunday and they're going to the cinema.

Why did I do that? Giggles, of course. But also because I'm ridiculously happy. That kid of mine has always struggled with social interaction, so this? This is huge. Massive. Monstrously marvellous. And I want the world to know. I want to hire skywriters and rent a parade float!

But I can't. And so, for now at least, shouting in our cul-de-sac car park will have to suffice.

Do the weird stuff *(so long as it doesn't get you arrested)*, and let the crazy out of the box... I *love* that saying, by the way. It started a while back, when I was teaching my son about boundaries, about when and where it was ok to be full-on, and when it was better to rein it in, just a little.

Does it offend people? Absolutely! Especially in the post office queue with a bunch of old biddies who couldn't mind their own business if their pension depended on it.

But does it work for my son? Hakka Noodles, yes! And way better than some dull, ten-minute lecture on *'appropriate behaviour'* and the *'consequences'* of not following the rules... *Blah, blah, blah.* With just the thought of that, my soul begins to wilt *(not unlike the bathroom plant, Florence, which was apparently foolproof. Turns out not so much!)*

No, I don't need to fry my son's brain with a list of regulations to abide by. He knows where my line is, and he respects the half-joking, half-whip-cracking tone that bellows from within whenever he wanders too close.

You know the one - it starts with their first name. Not a nickname or the shortened version that we, as brand-new parents, vowed never to use, but the full name, with every syllable declared. And when things get really serious, their middle, subsequent, if given, and last name are summoned like the devil to a tea party on Elm Street.

"ALBERT BARRY CHARLESTON!"

(That's not my kid's name by the way - it just amused me to write the whole 'A B C' thing. It's the little things in life!)

No, I actually prefer to call out really embarrassing stuff, especially to my almost teenage daughter. *Snoodle Plum, Chicken Dinner, Reggae Reggae Sauce*, and our family favourite, *Bob.* Everyone's called *Bob* here. *Good Job Bob, Well Done Bob, Let's Go Bob, What Ya Doing Bob...*

It's a collective, a sign of belonging.
And we all need that, in some way or another.

I actually thought I was a bit of a lone ranger until I had kids...

Obviously, I found some kind of *'connection'* with their fathers *(multiple, well not multiple. One each - no judgment needed!)* But my children were the beginning of me, as much as I of them.

And when the soup hit the fan a few years back *(because profanity isn't always needed to paint a picture)*, I found out just how strong my need to survive really was. I won't bore you with the details *(well, not now at least),* but finding yourself in an almost destitute situation, with nowhere to run and nowhere to hide, well, it makes you ridiculously grateful for the 6am bed-jumping antics that only a three-year-old can deliver.

I couldn't be grumpy or mad at the world, with his beaming smile, catching the morning light. Day after day, he would wake me with *"Mama! Mama!"* as if we'd been separated for months, not mere hours. And five years later, he still looks at me in a way that warms my heart. The kind that makes time pause and reminds me that I do exist in the best possible way.

On the days when my glass feels half empty, he doesn't just refill it - he overflows it, with laughter, bear hugs, and an enthusiastic twenty-minute info dump about obscure kitchen gadgets he's seen on TV. It's like adding a metaphorical paper umbrella and sparkler stick, and turning an ordinary moment into something worth celebrating.

I am grateful for those days. No scrap that - I'm grateful for every day, even the ones that start with 07:56 pull-up duty calls and end with fifty-seven reasons why he's not yet ready for bed.

I'm even *sort of* grateful for the teenage mood swings my daughter has brought to the table. At times, it's like having a sleepy dormouse on board, only it has bipolar, a sweet tooth, and the ability to verbally rip your throat out for questioning their recent life choices…

Ok, that *may* have been a slight overkill, but teenagers do often bring drama to the dance, so it kind of fits! Besides, my daughter is rarely offended by my nonsense. She might call out a shocked *"Mum!"* now and then, but we'll soon fall about laughing, as though we're both twelve, and the best of friends.

And honestly, that's part of *my* survival too. Because some days, it's the little moments, shared laughter, inappropriate jokes, and the sheer absurdity of life, that keep me going.

It's not just about getting up in the morning, finding some semi-clean clothes, and making peace with the 3% battery life on your phone... *Because who knows where the one remaining charging cable has gone!*

It's also about accepting that some days your to-do list might remain *to-do'd*. You'll serve chips for dinner, shout into the fridge, all while having a meltdown because the sink is clogged with hair, again.

And that's fine. That still counts.

You don't have to sparkle.
You don't have to be inspiring.
You just have to do your best, preferably in pants, but that's up to you.

That was your happy vibes paragraph, by the way. Soak it up. Because from here on in, the book descends into chaos, questionable decisions, and stories I probably shouldn't be writing.

But I'm going to anyway. You're welcome.

Chapter 2: Sugarcoating

From diagnosis to rainbow cupcakes
and emotional whiplash – no filter applied.

I am a serial sugarcoater. I will sugar the shellfish out of that bad news, those harsh truths and unfair realities… for my kids. Anyone else can take it like a hooker in Amsterdam.

But, when my son, who, as you're probably aware by now, is not yet toilet trained, unleashes the inevitable, I am not afraid to tarnish my sugarcoating persona.

"Good cod, I think something crawled up there and died!" is probably my most-used response. And it's often said from beneath my jumper, as I bury all of my senses deep down… *(Believe me when I say, the down does not go deep enough!)*

I'm thinking I probably should have given some kind of disclaimer at the start of this chapter for people with weak stomachs or nervous dispositions. Sorry about that. But in my defence, the introduction does come with a warning. And for future reference, that should be applied to *every* chapter!

For parents in a similar situation, this will make perfect sense. Whether you're lucky enough to have support from the specialists or not *(we are not),* the struggle is real. And the end, somewhat unimaginable.

But this chapter isn't about my son's monthly pull-up orders. Or how after eight years *(almost thirteen if you count my eldest, who was potty trained at three. And yes, she knows I just shared that with the world!)*, I'm still deeply and *profoundly* offended by all things bathroom-related.

FYI – for those of you who casually share a bathroom with your partner, door ajar like it's a casual drop-in centre... I don't know how you do it.

The "Let's chat about the MOT" while someone's mid-flush vibe? Or the rock, paper, scissors round to decide who's going back downstairs to take tomorrow's chicken out of the freezer, *while seated*? That's a level of closeness I simply can't aspire to. If you're holding eye contact and holding toilet roll at the same time, I'm out. Fully out!

No, this chapter is about sugarcoating. It's about how we soften the sharp edges of the world for our kids, how we wrap the truth in rainbows and unicorns just to make it a little kinder. And try our best to keep the monsters at bay.

But the thing about sugarcoating is... It only really works when you're the one doing it.

When the specialists gently told me my son had Autism, four years ago now, I cried. Not a quiet, dignified tear, but the kind of raw, deep sobbing that takes over your whole body. I remember pulling into a layby after that first meeting, gripping the steering wheel, and letting it all out…

How could they possibly know after just two hours?
How could they sum up my child, my beautiful, brilliant boy, with a diagnosis that felt so heavy I could barely hold it?

But the truth is, for us, it *was* that clear-cut. His traits, his differences, had been there since very young, written in bold, flashing lights. I just hadn't let myself read them. Maybe I didn't want to… Maybe I was too scared to.

Then came the list, the extras, the additional needs of Autism. And it hit me so hard that I thought my heart was going to break, right there in the car.

The worst, I think, the most gut-wrenching for me, was the delayed language development. I'd always believed he was super bright, singing his ABCs at two, and mimicking his big sister for endless giggles.

But it turned out he had no real understanding of the words. Because Echolalia, the involuntary repetition of words and sounds, had just masked the problem so well, it went unnoticed.

He wasn't *communicating* - he was simply echoing the world around him.

Even now, four years later, I can feel the emotions swell up inside, as I relive the days after my son's initial CAMHs meeting. The team was incredible - they saw my pain, my internal battle, but gently guided me toward seeing the diagnosis through, for *his* sake.

Unfortunately, it took another two years for the official paperwork to arrive, thanks to one house move and one less-than-supportive worker dragging her feet.

And then, one day, it arrived on my doormat.

I spent the following days wrestling with how to tell my son. In my heart, I knew I had to tell him. All of his '*All about me*' meetings, as we called them, had to have a meaning. And on some level, he had to understand, to make sense of who he was.

In the end, I baked rainbow cupcakes, threw a mini party in the living room, presented an Autism Superhero book, and declared to friends and family on social media that we finally had *"big news"*, as if I were announcing the arrival of a new puppy, rather than a lifelong diagnosis.

Why I thought *that* was the best way to handle it, I honestly don't know. Maybe it was the emotional equivalent of trying to plug a leaking pipe with glitter and good intentions. A panic response in party form.

I think I was just desperate to make it feel OK, for him, and maybe even more so for me. But he didn't need it. He didn't need that frantic comforting. And in my heart, I should have known that. Over those two years, his understanding and communication with the world had grown massively. And like a hero *(not a book hero but my hero)*, he took it all in his stride.

And I just stood there, completely floored. Because I'd spent so long building it up in my head, the how, the when, the what ifs, convinced it would break him. But it didn't. It broke me, if anything. The relief. The guilt. The knowing I'd tried so hard to protect him from something he already had the strength to carry.

We try so hard to shield our kids by softening the truth, by holding back just enough to make the world seem safer. But maybe we're really just trying to soften it for ourselves. Because the hardest part isn't what they face - it's the ache in our chests as we watch them face it, wishing we could throw ourselves in front of every sharp edge.

I'm honestly feeling so emotional writing this chapter. I don't think the gentleness of the music playing on my headphones is helping, or the dim lights. But…

"Mum, you know the song 'Nom Nom Nom Nom' by Paragrip? I've found a piano version on my game. And I've made a level with it!" is today's random interruption.

Safe to say, my emotional bubble is now burst!

I love that kid so much. He has the best, and the worst, but mostly the best timing.

There are some things I choose *not* to sugarcoat with my kids. Case in point - having read the start of this chapter, my almost teenager now knows what a *'Hooker in Amsterdam'*; is. And, according to her *(who was at that point in a state of hysterical laughter),* it's wildly inappropriate.

News flash, kid - that's half the fun of writing it!

And yes, before anyone points it out, I'm fully aware that telling my young, impressionable daughter this was *also* wildly inappropriate. But have you *met* Google? Have you seen how eager, sassy, and downright *loose-lipped* she gets after two Tequilas and a packet of nuts?

(Sorry - that was a lot of stereotyping. I have no idea what Google identifies as. Or if they have a nut allergy. My bad!)

Let's face it - the world is far too accessible, no matter how well we lock down the loaded guns, or at least tell ourselves that we have. And so, I would rather have those inappropriate conversations with my child firsthand. I may not win *'Parent Of The Year'* awards, but I'll sleep a little easier knowing that my daughter is both educated and mortified in equal measures.

I would include my son in that statement, but at this stage in life, he's doing his best ostrich impression - excitable, ignoring the facts, and likely to burst into tears and/or laughter at any given moment. Plus, nothing really mortifies him, other than paint, Nutella, or unknown sticky substances on his hands.

One thing my daughter did ask about the book was, why am I using hookers, drugs, and parties on Elm Street *(previous chapter)* to... Actually, let me rephrase that.

Why am I *referencing* hookers, drugs, and parties on Elm Street, but then omitting every swear word, and replacing it with some ridiculous alternative?

A fair question.

It might seem strange, but for me, the F-bomb really lacks substance. It's been so overused, like car bumper stickers in the '60s, that it's lost all its punch. These days, it's less of a linguistic grenade and more like an angry Yorkshire Terrier yapping at your ankles. Annoying? Sure. Impactful? Not so much.

That, and my children, particularly my son, will tell me off for even a hint of shi… which is ironic, given his frequent *Eau de Unearthed Dead Warthog* aromas!

He's such a rule-led stickler… Well, mostly, until he's not! Take, for example, a few days ago when he was slipping and sliding in the bathtub. Hearing the high-pitched giggles, I called through from my office, *"Don't mess around in there!"*

"I can't hear you" was the reply I got, in his best SpongeBob voice impression, so I tried again, and again.

After the third attempt, he got *"STOP BEING A TIT IN THE BATHROOM!"* which seemed to make a more lasting impression.

Sugarcoated? Yes, otherwise I'd have said something like, *"Are you actually wanting my foot up your backside, because that level of craziness sure sounds like an invite!"* I'd never say that. I'd definitely think it. And I'd say it in my head. But I'd try *really* hard not to let the words come out to play.

That being said, *'Tit'* has become an officially mum-acceptable word to use. I may say it. They may laugh at it. But they can't use it in context other than "*Oh look at that lovely bluetit out the window!"*

Yes, I gave my son an actual, legitimate sentence to use the word in, as without it, my days would be consumed with a barrage of *"Can I use the word 'Tit' in this sentence?"* Believe me when I say, we've been there before. The *silent K* at the start of *Knight and Know* stole many a happy hour from me back in 2022. My son became obsessed, and I mean utterly obsessed, with adding the inconspicuous letter to any words that he saw fit. And I had to explain, like a stuck Rick Astley record, that he can't just change how words are spelt, no matter how valid his argument.

There are indeed times, not many, but the odd occasion, when my son needs to listen, accept, and move on. But those moments usually rank high on his internal *'Does Not Compute'* list, along with, "*Why does ASDA need to have three bins so close to each other? That's just an extreme amount of bins! Whoever decided that three bins that close to ASDA didn't really think about it. They just put them there. And left!"*

And, one of my personal favourites, "*Why haven't you stopped for fuel? The light is on and you need to get fuel before you run out! Mum, you need to find fuel urgently!"* For clarity, I still had twenty-seven miles left on the clock, eight miles to drive, and precisely zero miles worth of enthusiasm to stand in -1°C temperatures at 8pm, wrestling with a frozen petrol pump.

But my son doesn't get that. To him, the fuel light coming on means immediate action. Not in five miles. Not when it's convenient. Now.

It's pure, unshakable logic. And logic, when ignored, can quickly spiral into a full-blown panic. His body stiffens, his voice rises, and the persistent, relentless *"But if you don't, the world is going to end!"* kicks in like a siren he cannot shut off.

Cue the increasingly dramatic countdown to…
what he believes will be…
our inevitable…
demise.

We interrupt this broadcasting for a much-needed shower, his, not mine, and almost head-butting burst of giggles, as my son's t-shirt flew off his head and into the already running water.

Life is rarely dull here. So when people ask, "Don't you get bored at home?" I struggle to keep a straight face.

Bored? When have I ever had time to be bored? My life is a never-ending tale of random conversations, today's being about Ralf the Cat, who needed an IV in the vet hospital. FYI, I have no idea who Ralf is, or why he needed an IV.

There's a lost sock crisis, a hot glue gun demonstration going on in the kitchen (my almost teenage daughter is crafting something magnificent for sure), and an unexplained pile of coins on my desk. The cats know I'm late with their dinner... exactly two minutes late. And in approximately half an hour, some strange man is going to knock at my door to buy a treadmill that my ADHD no longer has interest in.

Bored? Chance would be a fine thing!

I wish I could sugarcoat the world for my son. I wish I could march up to every judgmental backseat life coach who stares when he, at eight years old, takes Fred Bear into the shops. Fred Bear, who helps my boy to feel that bit safer, when the world is too loud, too fast, too much…

And shove a sour lollipop straight into their gaping mouths! Preferably one that fizzes violently and glues their lips shut for a bit. You know, just long enough to give them time to reflect.

But, even without the security guards in ASDA against me, I know I can't. I can't wrap him in cotton wool forever, or pretend to him that the world is some beautifully accepting place because, well… It's just not.

We've become a nation of... *offendedness? Offends?* No, wait, *offenders..* nope, definitely don't mean that one! Let's just say, a nation full of people who are easily offended. Or, as the unvictimized among us might say... Snowflakes!

A nation of *"Something's slightly displeased me, so I'm going to publicly rant about it. And if that doesn't work, I'll start a social media protest event with a hashtag and a Canva-made infographic!"*

From the outside, this *'delicately'* named *(with just a pinch of lavender and a smidgen of feelings-first fragility)* Woke generation appears to be organising *a cult-like brigade to 'Fend off the Zombies of Immorality!'* And yet, most of them can't even use a can opener, let alone make a positive dent in society.

I know - I'm just overflowing with wrongfulness here! But as much as I poke fun at these *(and many other)* situations, what I lack in political correctness, I like to think I make up for with love, laughter, and a bucket load of *'Life is too short to get hung up on that!'*

And this is probably where the real hate for me is going to start...

Yes - life *is* far too short to be offended by tattoos, music taste, relationship goals, actual meat-filled burgers, or pronouns that didn't even exist the last time I cleaned behind the fridge.

And no, I'm not going to start every conversation by asking Tom, Danielle, or Harry what titles they're vibing with this week, or whether my moo-filled milkshake is oppressing their oat-based lifestyle choices.

I mean, I could, but in return, I'd expect a full Q&A session. I'd want them to ask my profession *(if I hadn't already announced it like a cage fighting showdown)*, shoe size, dating history from 2001 to 2007, childhood pet trauma, the snack I'd choose in a unicorn apocalypse, long-term goals, allergies, and of course, uncensored views on canal boats.

Get a grip, fruit loops. As much as you've got every right to do your thing, however glitter-drenched, kombucha-fuelled, or morally inconvenient it might be, I've got the same right to do mine.

And so does my son, which is why I'll never ask him to zip up his Autism or downplay his ADHD to fit someone else's beige rulebook on *'acceptable behaviour.'*

Instead, I'm going to do my best to prepare him. To teach him to laugh,

to roll with the punches, to see the ridiculousness in life rather than letting it crush him. *(Although, I might hold off on letting him read all of my rambles until he's a bit older. No need to send his little mind spiralling down my personal wormhole of chaos just yet!)*

And sure, we may have to *'Put the crazies back in the box'* now and then *(still amusing me!)* But the box is never locked or hidden away. My son gets to be exactly who he is - weird, wonderful, and sometimes wildly inappropriate *(no idea where he gets that from)*, but always *himself.*

And honestly? That's more than good enough for me.

Side note: *For the record, I respect every human's right to live a full, glorious life, in whatever way fits them best. Gender, identity, lifestyle choices - I'm not here to judge anyone's ride. I'm just trying to survive mine, often with a moo-filled milkshake in hand.*

I'm not for or against anyone - I am Canada. I sit peacefully in the middle, cold from the outside in, but as polite as Geoff from HR.

So let's agree on this: mutual respect or bust.

Chapter 3: Sticky Notes

When the post-it says more
than the specialist ever did.

Me: *How much do you love me?*
Him: *To the moon and back*
Me: *But what if you forget to love me?*
Him: *I'll write it on a sticky note*

And he has, several times. Not because my boy worries he's going to forget to love me - that's a *ridiculous* suggestion!

No, it's because he sees how it melts my heart. And he's such a softy, such a genuinely kind and empathetic soul, which is pretty amazing given that the specialists told me, on several occasions, that "*Autistics don't feel emotions like they should, so don't expect much from him.*"

I beg your pardon?

Specialists are the ones who don't feel anything, or at least not many of the ones I've met. They seemed to be detached, and cold-natured flesh-dwellers, who sit ticking boxes as if they were playing some sort of diagnostic bingo.

"Super Stims - five has flexi limbs!"
"Clumsy Bumping - twenty-two is a jumping!"

I know this isn't always the case. In fact, we *do* have a lovely paediatrician right now - one whose soul hasn't yet been completely drained from her body. She's kind and compassionate, and her office is full of colour and life... *Unusual!*

But over the years, the lack of hope from other practitioners has been crushing. Cold, clinical voices echoing the same empty phrases. *"Don't expect this,"* or *"Don't expect that."* And each one landed like a punch to the gut, chipping away at the future I'd imagined for my beautiful boy.

I wanted answers, reassurance, *something* to hold onto. But all I got were warnings, limitations, and a handful of outdated leaflets that were supposed to tell me how to understand my child. As if *he* could be summed up in a three-fold pamphlet. Come on. I'm writing an entire book about my son, and even that barely scratches the surface!

But these sticky notes? *They* capture my son and his extraordinary world perfectly.

He doesn't like pencil work, not for the most, but he writes these for me.
He doesn't like the sticky feeling behind those squares of paper, but he'll touch them for me.
He finds it hard to express emotions, to find the right words, but these, these are perfect to me.

And he still points them out, held to the fridge by a magnet, every time he sits on the kitchen stool.

"Do you remember when I wrote those for you? Do you remember me writing that I love you? And that I always will?"

Stick that in your tick box, *Dr. Dry Toast with a Pinch of Pickle!* And yes, that's *exactly* how I imagined that particular specialist's *special* life to look.

In my head, he resides in a soulless, clinical box, masquerading as a home. The walls, a washed-out shade of beige, would suck the joy from your bones. Perhaps a single brown chair, identical to those found in a doctor's waiting room, would sit in the centre, stiff and unwelcoming, and perfectly positioned for staring into the void.

The air would undoubtedly reek of Dettol and despair. And his pet goldfish, a *'friend'*, dressed as a specimen for psychological research, would bob around in the corner of the room, unaware of the nullness around him...

Of course, I could be wrong. *Dr. Dry Toast with a Pinch of Pickle* might actually spend his weekends frocked as Brittany - an '80s call girl with a flowing blonde wig, and stilettos that make your eyes water.

Now, there's an image you *didn't* need!

I'm not a fan *(in case that wasn't yet obvious)* of the clinical drivel that my son and I have often had to endure. I find it insulting for the most, condescending, and of little to no help. And I guess that plays a part in why we chose to home-educate.

I never wanted either of my children to feel boxed in. To me, the idea of them being crammed into a rigid system and expected to conform felt...suffocating. They would have to *fit in*, to mould themselves into something more *acceptable*. And in doing so, they would lose the very things that make them *them*.

With my son trying to make sense of the world through Autism and ADHD, and my daughter battling the quiet but relentless grip of social anxiety, the traditional school path felt less like an opportunity and more like a setup for struggle. A place where they'd be misunderstood, where they'd have to shrink themselves just to survive.

And I couldn't do that to them. I *wouldn't* do that to them.

So, I chose a different path.

Hang on. Me? Do something different? Break away from the norm? Rebel against society? I know - shocking! I mean, it's not like this book is built on *exactly that* premise. It's not as if I'm sat here on a Thursday afternoon, covered in tattoos, with long grey highlighted hair (yes, I am ageing disgracefully!), a coffee in one hand, and a tick list of inappropriate notes in the other.

And let's not forget about the poised highlighter, ready to *strategically* mark the words most likely to get me banned by the social media overlords... Bring on the emojis, I say, to outdo their slithering bots of righteousness! For I shall reign inappropriateness, and make you snigger when you know you shouldn't! I shall bring tears of laughter, and whispers of '"What the Halloumi?!"...

Gotta love some squeaky cheese!

Anyway...

I've lost my train of thought a little here. Actually, no - the train has fully departed whatever station I was parked at. And I can just about see it in the distance, puffing away with zero intention of returning.

People talk about baby brain like it's a phase, a temporary side effect of the jumble-sale style hormones, like it'll vanish the moment you sleep for more than three hours or remember what day it is without checking the bin schedule.

Mine? They set up a beanbag, opened a snack drawer, and decided to stay.

Questions I never thought I'd have to answer swarm my days like a protest of angry bees. Why are they protesting? Because I dared to spread their honey *3mm* thick on the bread instead of *2.5mm*. Or maybe because the sun is directly in their flight path, and I *failed* to provide them with a timely weather briefing.

Yes, life really can be *that* pernickety.

If you have a child whose logic outshines the bounds of normality, you'll know the battle isn't just about explaining things - it's about *proving* them. It's about navigating a world where facts reign supreme and feelings hold no weight. And where *your* reasoning is flawed simply because *theirs* makes more sense.

It's exhausting. I often get to the end of the day, mentally done from side-stepping every situation that could end in tears, his or mine. And some people will say that I'm mollycoddling him by doing so. That the world is harsh and unfair, and he just needs to *learn to deal with it.* That I'm doing him no favours by keeping the realities at bay.

But to those people, let me ask you this.

Did you believe in Santa as a kid?
Did the Tooth Fairy leave you pennies under your pillow?
And did the Easter Bunny deliver chocolate eggs while you slept?

Did your teacher encourage you to *reach for the stars* when you wanted to be an astronaut?

Or tell you that you had the *voice of an angel* in the school nativity when, in reality, it was less *heavenly choir* and more *tortured cat*?

I'm not saying we all grew up in a garden planted with encouragement, watered with love, and tended with faith and guidance. I sure as heck didn't. But I'm pretty certain that the brutal realities of how impossibly unfair life can be weren't stuffed into your Christmas stocking either.

Kids should be allowed to be kids, regardless of their needs and understanding of the world. They *should* be shielded from the harshest corners of the world and given time to grow wild with hope, curiosity, and impossible dreams. And my kid is no different, which is why I will, for as long as he allows, open those doors, sweep away the worries, and squeeze his hand tight as he walks the path ahead.

A wee heartwarming moment as I sit writing this chapter...

My son has come to join me in my gangway office (FYI, it's literally the upstairs landing, but it's a big landing. And it adopted a desk and Kallax unit, along with a load of other junk, when we moved in two years ago!)

He asked to sit by me and work on his cross-stitch bookmark. This is huge for us, not least of all because it's super fiddly. And my boy's fine motor skills are not always his friend.

Those struggles almost always end in frustration, with growling, grumping, and a general hatred for the rest of the world.

But this four-heart pattern, which he first started at some summer craft initiative last year and initially shunned, has won over his patience, one stitch at a time.

The concentration, along with absolute joy on his face, as he completes each little cross, is magical. And it reminds me of how immense these so-called small wins really are.

I think I might start living by those rules.

- ★ Got out of bed before 9am - go me!
- ★ Used my big girl words rather than grunting at fellow house members - win!
- ★ Found three of my 'missing' cups dotted around the house before mould set in - awesome!

I like it! I like it a lot!

Did I always know I'd end up writing a ridiculous, *perhaps* helpful, and *outrightly inappropriate* book in my 40s? Absolutely not. But oh, how I wish I had.

I wish I could've told my English teacher right then and there, or put it in my Record of Achievement folder for *'Future life goals'*. You know, the one we left high school clutching like some sacred relic, convinced it would *make or break* our future. The one we were told to bring to interviews because, apparently, our entire worth could be summed up in a laminated hardback with a few generic teacher comments…

Yes. That folder. The one most of us never saw again!

But, instead, my writing talent *(yes, I know - stretching it a bit there but we're going to roll with it anyway!)* was channelled into the *'thrilling'* world of social media marketing. For a number of years, I spent my days crafting riveting content for Chakra Fulfilment and Swimming Success for the Under-5s! Social media marketing at its *finest*, I kid you not.

…Ok, maybe not.

But words? They've always been there, lurking in the background like that one questionable jumper you can't remember ever buying. You don't know where it came from, it doesn't match a single thing you own, and yet, for reasons even you don't fully understand, you've kept it.

Maybe out of guilt. Maybe out of some irrational loyalty to the mothball-scented chaos of your past. Or maybe it's just in case Great Aunt Maggy shows up unannounced one day, clutching a tray of eggless sponge and asking if you still wear it *'for special occasions.'*

You won't.
You never have.

But there it is, still taking up space, much like your, I mean, *my* tendency to overshare...

It wasn't until life got a bit louder, messier, and a whole lot more intense that the writing started to matter. That's when it stopped being a means to an end and started keeping me up at night. Like a half tub of ice cream, that I wasn't emotionally prepared to commit to but somehow ended up finishing anyway.

And no, it wasn't even *my* story that pushed me into this mess - it was my son's. Because sometimes life hurls something at you so big, so maddeningly relentless, that if you don't let it out, it'll leak out sideways anyway. Through rants. Or fridge crying. Or shouting at printers.

So here I am, pouring my heart onto these pages. Not because I've got it all figured out - crikey, I haven't even mastered the art of keeping the bin from overflowing!

No, it's because I know what it's like to be knee-deep in the chaos and still wondering if you're doing enough. And if anything I write makes just one person feel even a smidge less bonkers, less broken, less alone on this cracked-up parenting rollercoaster... then praise the lopsided llama, for I am your emotional support author!

Feeling like a hero. Looking more like a homeless crackpot, squatting in the depths of my office with an unintentionally cold coffee and yesterday's hair nest for my troubles... But ya know, still winning at life!

I was *going* to write some inspirational speech here about *"Looking around and seeing the great success you are."* But then I actually *looked* around… and saw a rogue roll of wrapping paper from *who knows when*? A packet of needles (*sewing, not drugs!*), and *two* sets of bathroom scales on the floor. *(For the record, I was convinced the first set was lying to me. Turns out… it wasn't. Rude.)*

So, we'll scrap that *motivational nonsense* and instead, insist that you find, or, failing that, *buy* yourself a pack of sticky notes. Personally, I have several, my favorite being the *cute* cat butts in fluorescent pink. Yes, I am that childish!

I have also seen several packs with *'explicitly encouraging'* words stamped across the top. However, given that I have *dustbin lids* on the loose *(guess who's been teaching the kids cockney rhyming slang today!),* anything that screams *"Keep f**ing going!"* is probably *not* the best choice.

Your situation may be different. But mine bears the wrath of a 4ft-nothing sergeant major, who will echo the "*No Bad Words"* drill until I'm forced to eat the fruitful sticky notes, just to destroy the poisonous evidence.

But anyway… Why do you need sticky notes? Well, let's start with

- The obvious note-making scenario - yes, we're going back to basics, because apparently yelling *"remind me later"* into the void isn't a reliable filing system.
- A designated mug spot for those of us who believe in coasters but don't have one to hand.
- A good cover-up for when you ignored the precious point and now have a guilt-ridden stain on your desk or side table.

But wait, there's more!

- A tactical *'Do Not Disturb'* forehead label - ideal for Monday mornings, post-school runs *(woohoo for home-ed and dodging that chaos!),* or when a child decides right now is the time to ask, *"Mum, do clouds have bones?"* while you're one eyebrow pencil stroke away from losing it.
- A helpful reminder for your older children - slap that bad boy *(the sticker, not the child)* onto their laptop with "CHORES BEFORE SNORES" in bold caps, since verbal reminders, texts, calendar alerts, and interpretive dance routines have all failed.
- A fake *'important memo'* for your desk - looks totally professional on Zoom, but actually says, *'This meeting could've been an email,'* or *'Mentally unavailable. Please consult a potato.'*

But for me, the most important role of the humble sticky note is the space and autonomy it gives my son. It's not so big that it's overwhelming, nor too small that it restricts his thoughts. It's just enough, enough for him to get his words out in a way that feels safe.

And I love that. Because giving our kids the tools to *express* themselves, to *communicate* their feelings is invaluable. It's not just about talking - it's about building a place where they *can* talk. A harbour where they know they can rest for a while, unload what they need to, and trust that whatever they share will be met with dignity and respect.

Is that always easy? Absolutely not. And honestly, I had no idea just how uneasy it could feel until I found myself parenting my daughter, who has social anxiety, and my son with delayed communication skills.

Actually, no. Scrub that. It was *my* communication skills that were delayed. Not just because I grew up in a household that didn't talk, but because I had to unlearn everything I thought I'd figured out, which was a tough pill to swallow.

I also had to learn how to give my kids a safe space, without wading in with my overbearing, overemotional, and overprotective Mum boots on.

Size five and a half, in case you were wondering. I know you probably weren't, but I'm an active oversharer. And we haven't had a random blurtation for a while, so there it is, like an extra gherkin to ruin your lunch!

You're welcome!

They don't always talk… No, that's not true. My son always talks. All day long, he rabbits on, but usually about his current obsessions. Or he'll be echoing and stimming like a podcast on double speed - one that you didn't subscribe to, can't pause, and is mostly about kitchen gadgets and obscure pollution facts.

My almost-teen daughter, however, could easily go six hours without speaking to another human being, longer if drinks are delivered at regular intervals and no one makes eye contact.

Obviously, I don't just leave her to rot in her hoodie-cave of solitude. No. I coax her out with offerings, usually snacks, sometimes memes, and the occasional, *"Come see the stupid thing I just did!"* shouted like I'm promoting a sold-out comedy special.

And we WhatsApp… from my office to her bedroom. In the same house. Because apparently, physically entering her space is now considered an act of war. If I so much as step inside her doorway without a solid reason, I'm met with a look that suggests I've kicked a puppy and betrayed the entire village.

Sure, I *could* roll my eyes. I *could* insist she just climb the stairs to my office, like a normal human, and talk to me with her mouth instead of her thumbs. But I don't.

Because if messaging me from two rooms away is what makes her feel safe, if it gives her the space to say what she's thinking without the burning anxiety of being *'on the spot'*, then I'll meet her there. In the digital void. With emojis, GIFS, and the occasional *"Did you take your glass through yet?"*

And honestly? If I ever need a little more face-to-face action, I'll just change the Wi-Fi password and wait for her to come find me.

***FYI**: I'll likely be lying under my bed, trying not to giggle and hoping the orange-flavoured wildebeest doesn't rat me out with his demands for attention!*

Notes From the Edge

3rd February 2025 ♡

This cup contained
all of my people skills!

No, I couldn't be bothered to get a plate.
Yes, I was sitting in the kitchen with my jam on toast.

Why? Because one sofa, having fallen victim to a split coffee, was offering sweet promises of dampness, whilst the other was, as usual, occupied by my son and his "Do not move my teddies" brigade. And no, this was nowhere near enough coffee to people today. Nowhere near enough.

In other news, the cereal was "too plain", the straw, unfindable, and 10:17am, too early to get dressed. I knew from the off it was going to be 'one of those' Mondays, and lo and behold (fun fact – I spent years calling that 'wo and behold'. And only realised my mistake after Googling how to spell it!), the day did not disappoint.

Or rather, it did, but in a totally non-surprising way.

Music Monday 𝄞⨾𓍢ִ໋🎧 Magic Monday ☆₊˚.⋆☾⋆⁺₊✧ Yeah, no. More like *Massive Meltdown Monday*, complete with misery, mayhem, and the misreading of what should have been a simple situation. I repeat. Should have.

The morning disappeared before I could get a grip on it, and suddenly I was flapping around like a chicken who'd just spotted her Uncle Derek featured in a KFC special.

I've been taking my son to piano lessons every single Monday for the past 18 months. It's always been at midday. And it's always been a 15-minute drive away from my house. So, quite why I was so under-prepared today is anyone's guess!

The lesson went well for the first 10 minutes – my son recited his scales like a pro (not that I would expect anything less, given the rinse-and-repeat formula they bring to his life) and I sat in awe as he...

No, that's a lie. I jotted down notes on my phone for the next chapter of the book ✎﹏ Apparently, my logical black-and-white rule led child (except for when he's not) has found God! And when I say 'God', I mean, we parked outside the local church and their banner 'inspired' his faith.

What the humming cauliflower?
What the actual frenzy of jelly beans has a banner got to do with thinking "I might try to be religious"? I mean, way to go on the graphic design skills – I completely applaud this. But, seriously? "I might try to be religious"?

No mate.
Your life is complicated enough.

I fully support your love of music, your cries for help with anything that has a plug, and your pull-up shower-downs. But we're not heading down that road. I mean, it's already hard enough to make sense of the living, the here and now, without adding in a subscription plan to the afterlife.

And no, before you ask, or disown me for being a Militant Atheist, it's not that I'm against religion. I get that, for many people, it's a source of comfort - something to hold onto when life gets rough. Like Scouts. Or AA meetings.

It's just not for me. And until my kids have formed brains bigger than pea farts, I'd rather they left it be too. Let's be honest - between pre-teen hormones and my emotionally charged ostrich of a child, life is already blowing raspberries in my face 🌀.'

Anyway, despite the pre-class theological debates, my musical genius continued to play well. I swear he felt that beat deep within. And really connected with the piece.

Since dismissing the idea of exams anytime soon, his whole attitude has relaxed. And he's found his happy place again, right there at the piano. Or, at least it was until Mr D asked him to go beyond his comfort zone. And piece together the short bursts of music he'd been playing so beautifully.

Now, in a different lesson, time or universe, this would have excited my son.

But not today. Today, this was too much. The expectations were set too high. And the internal pressure that he so obviously felt began to flow with tears, and stammering, and feet shaking as they dangled from the stool.

My heart truly aches for this kid. All I could do was pull him in close and hold him. Though Mr D and I did our best to shift the mood, to salvage what was left of the lesson, the bubble had already burst. The energy, the momentum, gone. And my son, normally so full of life, was now lost in the weight of it all.

Urgh. I hate days like this...

On the drive home, windows down and in car beats on repeat, the frustration began to fade. With his fingertips poking out over the window ledge, my boy let the cold air rush across his hand. The car read 4°C, but watching him get lost in that little slice of sensory therapy? That warmed me.

I wish I had that get-out-of-jail-free card that he carries around. I wish I could opt out when things get tough, and allow the moment to absorb me like he does. But instead, I'm here, trying to navigate the ups and downs as best I can. And today has been full of them.

His lunchtime toastie was *almost* a complete fail, betrayed by its oddly unfamiliar *togetherness*, despite being made of individually acceptable ingredients. My fault entirely (though, on a *good* day, I'm convinced it would have been a massive hit!) But Yum-Yums seemingly restored his faith in mankind, and more so, in me.

The new cup, on the other hand, was a definite disappointment. It didn't look *exactly* like the label suggested. But the pre-planned painting (because we don't just DO that kind of stuff) was fun, in that I did all the messy stuff and he watched from the table's edge with a safety wet wipe in hand.
I guess today wasn't the day.

I guess I misread the warning signs. And now, I feel terrible that I allowed him to emotionally crash.

I am that kid's safe place. His go-to. His comfort. But sometimes, I get it wrong. Sometimes, I push too hard, miss the tiny details, the ones I *should* notice, the ones that matter most.

I'm trying, kiddo. I really am. I want to be everything you need, to catch you before you fall. And when I don't, when I misread those signs, or steer us in the wrong direction, know that I *feel* it too. I'm just as sad as you are, if not more so...

But all is not lost. The day was not a complete write-off, thankfully! And I am still my son's favourite person, which is just the best place to be -`♡´-

Also, three Good Things That DID Happen Today....

1) He asked for and ate 4 red grapes.
2) His new cutlery was a success, proved by the merciless hacking of potato stars!
3) And best of all, he's still singing. As I sit at what should be/used to be my tidy desk, which is now more of a tribute to parenthood and the coffee needed to survive it, I can hear him singing Christmas songs (in February) from the bath. And I couldn't be happier.

"You're allowed to scream, you're allowed to cry, but do not give up." – Author Unknown

Chapter 4: Mirror Mirror

Raising him honestly,
because I wasn't.

✦✦✦ Welcome to the latest episode of ✦✦✦

"What Da Duck Do I SayTo That!?"

Today's challenge is a real brain-bender. Picture this:
Your child is starting to sense that they're, well... *different.*

Ding ding!

You, the ever-wise adult in the room (ha!), have spent years decoding their quirks, navigating the sensory minefields, and shielding them from the *"Just try harder"* brigade *(you know who I'm talking about!)* like a parental bodyguard in fluffy slippers.

But now, the million-dollar question looms…
How do you actually tell them? Let's look at your options:

A. *Hand them a pile of textbooks thicker than a Christmas edition of the Argos catalogue, explaining in excruciating depth, why their brain sends mixed signals. Bonus point for using a bunch of scientific terms!*

B. *Send them a pre-recorded message, ideally filmed in a leather armchair, to say, "Well, champ, this is it. You've got some odd conditions that will make life trickier, that's for sure. But cheer up! The world needs more offbeat wildcards to balance out the top-button-done-up, beige-loving types. You've got this!"*

C. Go for the gentle, compassionate approach. Sit them down face-to-face, outline some of the things that make them different, and reassure them that, whilst those things may feel overwhelming right now, you'll be right there, helping them navigate it all, like a co-pilot on this rollercoaster of existence. Add hot chocolate and marshmallows to taste.

D. Gloss over it entirely. That's a later problem. A not on your radar situation. Right now, just getting through dinner without a meltdown and surviving the bi-weekly hair wash night without the screams of a medieval exorcism is all you can handle.

Doo doo doo!
It's time to lock in your final answers!

✦✦✦ End of Round One ✦✦✦

I actually know parents who've used all of the above. Yes, even the textbooks. And that's ok, because every kid walks a different path. And those paths? Well, they need scenery that fits. Some kids thrive on cold, hard facts. Others need soft landings, gentle words, and a gradual unfolding of truths. There's no single right way to do this - only the right way for *your* child.

I personally went with C. And it caused the meltdown of all meltdowns. Not from my kid. No, he took it like an *absolute hero*. I was the one who fell apart.

For weeks, probably months prior, I wrestled with the decision to tell him. Even before the diagnosis landed in my lap, it felt like an overly stuffed weighted blanket - one that was too heavy, too suffocating, and stitched together with a thousand *what-ifs*.

What if telling him changed how he saw himself? What if I got the wording wrong? What if I made it worse?

I spiralled. I quizzed the online communities. I wrote lists upon lists of pros and cons, then rewrote them when the anxiety monster whispered, "*But have you considered this terrifying new possibility?*"

And I broke down over it. More often than my 2003 Vauxhall estate.

See, my childhood was built on untold secrets and well-intended lies.

My Dad, whom I absolutely adored, died when I was five years old. And I spent the next seven years drowning in the grief of it, missing him, picturing the life we should have had, clutching onto every tiny scrap of his memory...

Only at twelve years old, an ugly truth was dropped on me. Cold and callously, without warning or care.

"I don't know why you're still upset. He wasn't even your real father. That man left when you were nine months old. A baby. Got up one day, went for milk, and never came back."

Just like that - no warning, no context, not even a comforting cup of hot chocolate to soften the blow. The man I had grieved for my entire childhood? He was no longer mine to grieve.

But it wasn't just the loss of him - it was the betrayal of truth. The silence that was handed to me in its place. The stories I'd built, the memories I'd clung to, the certainty of who I was and where I came from. It was all gone.

That's the damage of lies, even the ones meant to protect. They don't just shatter truths - they shatter people.

And that's why I agonised over how to tell my son his story. I refuse to be the person who hands him a truth wrapped in barbed wire and calls it a gift.

Now, I've already talked about our diagnosis journey back in the *Sugarcoating* chapter, so I won't drag you through that emotional brick wall again. But what I *will* say is that when the paperwork finally arrived, I did what any last-minute, overthinking, emotionally broken Mama Bear might do...

I threw a party. I dug out balloons from the attic, baked rainbow-frosted cupcakes, and enlisted the help of his sister to make a card!

Looking back, it was probably somewhat unnecessary. And kind of an odd response to the situation (*that wasn't even a situation, until I turned it into an everlasting gobstopper of a now situation!)* But in that very moment, it felt like the right thing to do. And for my emotionally charged ostrich, it became a moment worth remembering.

I recently asked him about that day, if he remembers.

"I remember when we had a party when we found that I have Autism. We had rainbow cupcakes. And there was a Superhero book about Autism as well. It was a very good day. I learned about me and about how I have Autism."

Yeah, that melts my heart. That says, *Mama, you did the right thing. You marked the occasion, made it part of his life, and though it looks weird on the outside, it felt warm and fuzzy on the inside.*

Now we, as a family, get to talk about his Autism freely. About how it lets him hold onto childhood a little longer, how it wraps him in a world built from routine and wonder, where small joys feel bigger and last longer.

We talk about his ADHD, how it fuels his energy, and lets him *be* him. But also how it collides with his Autism, tangling the world around in contradictions. And about how simple things, things that should be effortless, like sorting a pile of clean clothes, suddenly become mountains.

We talk about his speech difficulties. His echolalia, his stutter that sneaks in when he's stressed or upset. And more recently, how he sees those struggles in other children.

That, *that* is something beautiful.

To see himself in others, to recognise even the smallest pieces of his own challenges, and find comfort in knowing he's not alone. He feels empathy, the very thing they told me he wouldn't have. The specialists, the books, the *'well-meaning but utterly wrong'* folk who insisted that,

"Autistic children don't experience empathy like you or I.
It's just not in their nature.
You need to come to terms with it."

Yes, those phrases were driven into my heart, stapled to every meeting, every evaluation, every *'helpful'* pamphlet thrust into my hands.

And yet, here he is, seeing his own struggles reflected in others. Noticing when another child stumbles over their story the way he does. When their frustration bubbles up because the words just won't come out right. And instead of looking away, instead of missing it like they all said he would… *he cares*.

I don't mean he's rushing over with hugs and grand declarations of understanding. That's not where he's at. But he does see them. He does stop and soften.

That *is* empathy. Raw, unfiltered, in its purest form. The very thing I was told he'd never have. And yet, even with all his challenges, all his delays, it's *right there*.

Cue the legion of outraged, marching in with their pitchforks of indignation and banners that read *'Real Autistic Children Can't Do That!'*, because apparently, my child's struggles don't count unless they match theirs, tear for tear, meltdown for meltdown.

Clearly, the neurodivergent gods made a clerical error when handing out diagnoses, because *if my child can feel empathy and connection, then he can't actually be autistic.* I must be fabricating it. Or at the very least, embellishing the truth.

And for my audacity to exist outside their carefully constructed spectrum-of-suffering scale, I should, of course, be strapped to the pyre and set ablaze, like a witch from the fifteenth century!

(Insert evil laugh and dramamtic music here!)

No, humans aren't always kind to each other. And let's be real, we're not always kind to ourselves either. I can name ten of my own self-confessed flaws *right now…*

1. I'm ridiculously lazy with cups - why wash one when there's a whole cupboard full of clean ones?
2. My timekeeping is tragic. Like, "*I'll be there in five minutes"* is just wishful thinking.
3. I constantly forget my almost-teen still needs the parent filter and just blurt out the inappropriate.
4. I ignore messages, then forget I ignored them, and then forget to reply at all. The cycle is endless.
5. I am completely irrational about food in my car - crumbs under bums? *Absolutely not!*
6. I snooze my alarm at least four to seven times. Every. Single. Morning.
7. I will not leave the house without a full face of makeup and, at the bare *minimum*, my hair in a *'looks intentionally messy'* bun.
8. My desk is the yin to my car's yang - a chaotic sheep tip of open pens, notes, plates, and yes, crumbs.
9. I take unnecessarily long baths at night to avoid going to bed, even though I know I'll regret it in the morning.
10. I care too much about people's opinions while simultaneously *not* caring at all - it depends on my mood, the moon glow, and my blood-to-caffeine ratio.

And that's just the top ten!

But can I name three good things about myself? Three things that I genuinely like, or feel proud of, that *don't* include my kids? Yeah… Erm. Hmmm, that's not so easy.

I would've thought I'd have nailed the whole *'look in the mirror and recite positive mantras*' routine by now. I did, after all, spend a solid year and a half writing for this American guy who wanted pages upon pages of self-care wisdom for his *'journey to inner harmony'* website, on which, I once wrote:

"It seems like there's always something holding you back, always an obstacle standing in your way. And, as you patiently will the lights to change, you can't help but wonder why life has to be so hard..."

But honestly?

Between the cats wailing outside the bathroom *(because how dare I pee before serving them breakfast)* and my almost-teen attempting to demonically summon her cereal bowl from the kitchen so she doesn't have to interrupt her bed-rotting session, my '*morning good vibes'* have about as much impact as a soggy inspirational quote coaster: technically functional, but mostly just sad and damp.

And I'd bet a hot cup of coffee that most of you have felt that way, too. Maybe recently. Maybe right now.

Now, I think this is where I'm supposed to throw in some inspirational nonsense. But honestly, your expectations are way higher than my ability to pep-talk you into feel-goodism.

What I *will* say, though, is that life is basically just an endless buffet of weird, sometimes unwelcome opportunities.

Not necessarily opportunities to change the daily chaos (because, let's be real, that spaghetti hoop meltdown in aisle five is happening whether you like it or not), but rather, opportunities to take on the challenge, find the ridiculous in the riot, and perfect the art of ignoring the judgmental side-eyes from Karen in produce.

You've got this! And I've got a train of thought to try and find again.

I certainly don't want my kids growing up dragging around some inner grudge-gremlin, some lifelong beef with anyone who dared breathe too loudly in their direction. Or worse, launching a full emotional war crime tribunal against the very person who published books about their toilet training saga in the name of *'relatable content.'*

No - I want them to enjoy life. To have the kind of days where they mess up and move on without dragging it behind them like a broken shopping trolley.

So, every night before bed, my emotionally charged ostrich is encouraged to name something happy. Just one small moment from the day.

The only rule? It can't be the "*yummy dinner*" he ate ten minutes ago, as thinking further back exercises his short-term memory. *(Yes, ten minutes ago is technically short-term, but it's a little too short. No mental star jumps required for that one!)*

We've been doing this for nearly three years now, almost every single day. And sometimes, it does ignite a furious meltdown when he can't remember if we left the house, or what he even had for lunch. There are times when he struggles to mentally retrieve that *fun time playing a game with Mummy*, or recall the moment when he fixed his own socks.

But for the most part, he finds beauty, or pride and happiness, in things that most people would gloss over.

"I'm happy because today, we got to choose some new cereal."
"I'm happy because I finally finished my train track and it looks epic."
"I'm happy because I tried chicken rice and I loved it!"

I like to think he's banking those happy moments, like dropping 2ps into a coin jar. And one day, he'll pick out his favourite one, his favourite memory, and smile a little brighter.

But in reality? I'm pretty sure his brain is wired up for bigger things than remembering the day he got a giant world map puzzle. Still, I can live in hope. In blissful, deluded false pretence. Like much of the rest of my life!

Take when I was ten or eleven, and *convinced* I wanted to be a truck driver. It seemed like the dream, getting paid to see the world in all its glory. But now? Now I won't even fly down to London, let alone rustle up an international visa.

No, I prefer to jump in the car and road trip it to the nearest beach. Take in the scenery, the fresh air, a hot chocolate or an ice cream, season depending. And then go home, to sweet creature comforts.

Judge all you like, but the whole *'going on holiday'* thing always fills me with dread. I see other people radiating excitement - the countdowns, the holiday shopping sprees, the giddy anticipation of escaping the daily grind.

Meanwhile, my reality is a whiteboard covered in frantic scribbles, a war room of logistics, and lists upon lists that never seem to end. Things I need to do three months before. One month before. Three weeks before. One week before.

And then, of course, the 48-hour emergency panic where I realize I can't find the cat's vaccination cards, I haven't asked the neighbor to put the bins out, or checked thirty-seven times that my son's favorite cup and cutlery set is already packed in the depths of the already overflowing car.

It's true.

While other people are happily planning scenic pit stops and Googling the best chippy near the seaside, I'm knee-deep in stress, juggling last-minute shopping, emergency car checks, and preemptively overpacking in case the British weather decides to throw a tantrum mid-trip.

The idea of a holiday is supposed to be freeing. A break from the grind. A chance to breathe a little easier. But for me? It's just reality with extra miles, different cutlery, and a higher-than-average risk of someone losing their mind over forgotten headphones.

Am I weird? Probably. But here we are, planning a trip to Cornwall this summer, with the excitement of a woman awaiting a root canal, except with more luggage, fewer painkillers, and a higher chance of needing therapy afterwards.

While writing this, my son is sat on the office floor, drawing pictures of a cat called Bill. Lovely, right?

Except Bill looks like he's been through a shredder. He's got bandages on what I believe is his ear, eye, and leg. And his backstory? Yeah, that's a mind-boggler you might need to sit down for.

Apparently, Bill is on three sacks of pills a day (not bottles, sacks), which means he can't go to work. And yes, he works... as a content writer. Because, well, obviously.

Can't think where he got that idea from... oh wait, that'd be me. I've been a content writer for nearly four years now.

Yes, believe it or not, people actually pay me to write for them. I know – wild! It's a job I both love and hate, and sometimes, love to hate. Because let's be real – some topics I'm asked to cover are so painfully dry, I get mental xerosis, just from the title. However, it pays... sometimes.

It's true – freelance work sucks more than bedbugs. But ya know, I'm going to make my fortune with this book. You're all going to love it, demand a sequel, and I'll be so wildly successful that I'll have queues stretching out the door at book signings.

Ha! A girl can dream.

As I sit here, pondering my next chapter, I find myself wrapped in a blanket of self-reflection... *Oh, that was unintentionally poetic!*

Yes, the stories I've shared, the memories I've unearthed, some of which I thought were buried so deep they'd never resurface, all stir something from within.

Some make me laugh. Others prod at old wounds I assumed had long since scarred over. However, they're all mine, woven into the patchwork being I am today.

This book has almost become a form of therapy, which wasn't exactly the plan. But here we are, cracking open the tin can of my past like some unhinged archaeologist on a caffeine high.

And while some of you may be wishing I'd steered clear of the whole rehab vibes, I have to say, there's something unexpectedly healing about it.

Because reflection isn't just about looking back - it's about noticing how far you've come without realising you were moving. It's a soul-hugging moment, the kind that lets you breathe a little easier, even if life itself still feels like a tornado of unpredictability.

So yes, this book has been unexpected in so many ways. But I'm rolling with it. And if you're still here, wading through the brain mush with me, then I guess you are too.

Thank you. For sticking with me. For indulging my ramblings. For not backing away slowly when things got a little too deep or weird or both.

It means more than you'll ever know.

Chapter 5: Guilt

Welcome to the shame spiral.
We have snacks.

Mum guilt is real.

It wakes me in the middle of the night, floods my face with ugly tears, and forces me into a relentless cycle of self-punishment that's hard to break free from.

Just the other day, my son, my at-times-awkward and argumentative son, was giving it his all to *"I don't understand"* his way through a maths workbook. The bar was set low *(challenges aren't avoided; they're just carefully fenced in with very realistic boundaries),* and the answers were well within his capabilities.

But unfortunately, he was just in one of *those* moods.

The kind of mood where I could say something is black and he'd argue it's midnight grey. I could say it'll take five minutes, but he'll make damn sure it takes six and a half.

Yes, some days, it feels like my boy is on an actual mission to wind me up. Like one of those mischievous monkeys up in the tree, throwing twigs at you with the precision of a scientific genius. And laughing, knowing full well there's absolutely nothing you can do about it.

But honestly, that's not the full story. Sure, he has moments where he loves to push buttons. Most kids do. But with him, it's more than that. It's frustration, bubbling over when the world stops making sense *(even though that exact same piece of the world lined up perfectly yesterday. Go figure!)*

It's like waking up in a parallel universe where the traffic lights have been replaced with interpretive dance, the rules are written in Morse code, and a council of mildly deranged pigeons is in charge of decision-making… And yet, somehow, *I'm* the problem.

Anyway, at that moment, I was feeling like a zombie princess. *(Why another ridiculous metaphor? Well, because even the most sleep-deprived, yesterday's-jumper-wearing, caffeine-addicted mums deserve to wear crowns. They're just a little... wonky at times. Maybe slightly askew, held together with a bobby pin and a desperate whisper of hope. But still, a crown nonetheless.)*

I genuinely thought I'd already navigated every twist and turn this single maths page could throw at me. I was sure I'd drummed in the not-so-well-hidden patterns of the nine times table, and that I'd given my son the tools to conquer this maths-defying mission. I was convinced, *convinced* that this would be the day. The day I could tick a box, pat myself on the back for achieving something vaguely educational, and not feel like I needed to crawl into a hole and nap for three days straight.

But do you know what happens after ten times nine? No? I'll tell you.

The sequencing pattern screws me right over. It doesn't just falter - it recoils. It spins on its heel like a pantomime villain, laughs in my face like a high school bully, takes my sombrero, and calls me *El Stupido!*

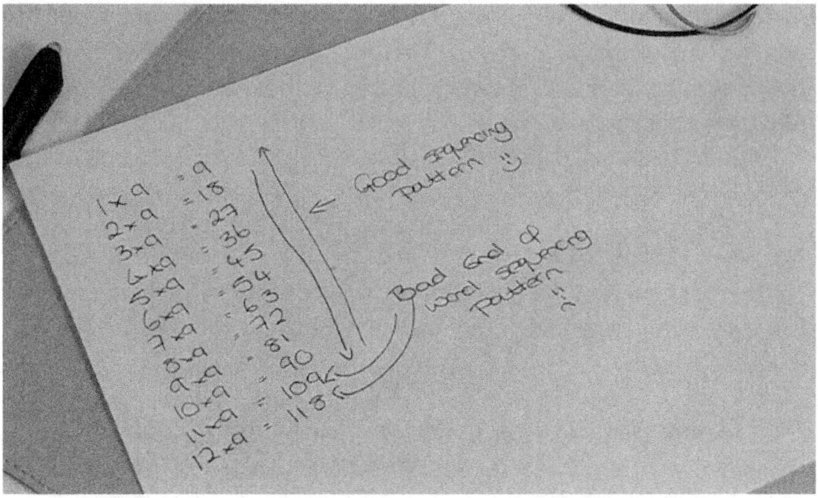

I wouldn't normally 'treat' you to such a fantastically mind-blowing diagram, but in this instance, I can't think how else to explain the 'agonising' problem my son had to face.

Also, the house is eerily quiet as the kids have been taken out, so I can write in peace, only, peace turns out to be somewhat deafening for me. Is it my ADHD? Maybe. My brain doesn't do well when it's not completely overwhelmed.

Or it could just be the empty echoes of my heart as my children have fun without me... No, no, the violins are not necessary! You carry on in your own bubble of ungrateful joy, like I'm not at home narrating my abandonment like a Victorian ghost with attachment issues.

However, this isn't actually where my Mum guilt boiled from though. No, this was just one of those things that could have so easily left him feeling like a maths genius, if only he'd been in the right mindset.

But he wasn't. And I accept that.

Instead, it was the panic attack that followed which broke my heart. My son got himself into such a state over the lack of logic, so overthrown by a world that suddenly didn't make sense, that his chest tightened, and breathing began to ache.

And I knew nothing of it.

Not when I called out his name.
Not when I repeated the answers, over and over, just to get it done.
Not even when frustration crept in, when he didn't come to me like I'd asked.

(Yes, I know I should've just gotten up and asserted my adulting expertise, but if we're being completely honest, we've all run out of parental energy before. We've all played the 'I'm busy' card, and insisted our kids use their teeny weeny legs to bring forth their troubles and woes at some point.)

No, I didn't realise until *after* I'd gone down to his learning space to find out what all the fuss was about.
Until *after* I'd led him upstairs to his room, his safe place, his sanctuary. Not as a punishment, never that. But as somewhere he could calm, reset, and be away from the noise of the world.
Until *after* I left him there, for five long minutes, thinking I was helping.

And when I went back up, that's when he told me.

Told me he hadn't been able to catch his breath, back in the learning space, when everything felt too much.
Told me he didn't know how to come to me, didn't know how to ask for help. He felt... stuck.

Right there. That's where Mum guilt punched me in the gut. Because, although he was fine and never in any real danger, I wasn't there when he needed me. And that? That will sit heavy in my heart for a long time.

Of course, being the absolute hero that he is, my son has long moved on from what happened. We learned a new sign *(Makaton is our go-to for tough situations)* to show if and when his chest feels tight again. And we agreed that if he needs help, he should go to the nearest person, even if that means barging straight into his sister's room so she can be his voice *(which she was obviously thrilled at… not! But understood why).*

It honestly leaves me in awe, knowing how resilient our kids can be, especially when they feel safe. And I know that despite what happened, my son does feel safe with me. He understands that I didn't know what was happening. That this was new territory for all of us. And that I'm sorry for not seeing the problem sooner.

Should I have been sat beside him the whole time? Pulled up a chair? Held his hand through the workbook? No. Absolutely not.

I know my son is, on the right day, more than capable and does not need a personal assistant to shadow his every move. And on a wrong day, he will muddle through at least some of the tough stuff, which is good enough for me.

And the silence is over. In ran the kids, full of ice cream, excitement, and empty gin bottles… lots of empty gin bottles!

No, they've not been on a pub crawl. It was a kind donation from a stranger on Facebook for my daughter to make Harry Potter-inspired potion with.

Never in the world would I, a teetotaler, have been able to fulfil my child's quest to carry out this art project, and yet, one stumbled across social media post later, and she's set up to add frog's eyes and cabbage to purple puffs of newt!

> *I feel guilty for a lot of things my kids have had to face. Some days it sneaks in, quietly. Other days it hits like a freight train.*

My mum not being around is a big one. A constant hum of failure in the background.

Because every child deserves grandparents. The kind that dote and spoil and tell wildly inaccurate stories about *"back in my day"* while slipping them a fiver for sweets. Don't get me wrong - she was never *that* grandparent. She wasn't even that parent. But still... I closed that door. Not for her, but *because* of her. And I'll never stop carrying the weight of that decision.

Guilt for chasing my dream. Writing. Creating.

The book, the work, the little corner of the internet where I pour my soul out and hope someone out there gets it. I could get a *'real'* job. One with a steady income, adult conversation, etc. But that would likely mean putting my kids in school and childcare. And I don't want to do that to them. Or me.

And the guilt for what I can't control...

Guilt for their Dads choosing not to be around, for me being insecure enough to need a full face of makeup before going out, for feeling sad over losses I've experienced. Big losses.

None of these things are really my fault. But I'm brilliant at convincing myself they are. I can cram all of it, *and so much more*, into a big old box labelled *'Things I should've got right'* or *'Things I screwed up beyond all hope.'* And then I carry that box, day and night, like a self-appointed guilt delivery service. Just in case I forget, for even a second, that I let the world around us get a little... tainted.

But before you start packing my bags for some hippy-happy healing retreat *(you know, the kind with overpriced yoga mats, group hugs, strangers chanting about self-worth under a full moon, and a woman named Sandrine trying to smudge my aura with ethically sourced sage),* let me set the record straight, by saying there *are* plenty of things I absolutely, unapologetically, *do not* feel guilty for, including:

- Blowing coffee-breath raspberries at my smallest child,
- Excessively cuddling my '*personal space'* eldest - she loves that one... not!
- Buying cats, despite our tenancy stating *a cat.* Singular.
- Eating a chicken sandwich at home ed meets, where the masses are preachy vegans.
- Buying a £40 log basket, or as I saw it, a super cute cat bed, for my feline friends to blatantly ignore.
- Using our multiple Alexas to summon my children, the husband (yes some poor sod actually wed me), next door's dogs, and potentially C.I.D. with my *'Alexa, how should I dispose of a body?'* requests... although none of them actually take any notice of my crazies.

I see all of that as balance. And finding balance, in my (*often not to be trusted but do in this case)* opinion, is what keeps us from falling off the merry-go-round of life.

Don't get me wrong - that doesn't make it *easy* or *convenient*. There will always be storms to ride out. And occasionally, my horse likes to rock from side to side, rather than glide up and down like every other pole-impaled pony.

In that one sentence, I've seemingly taken a princess-inspired dream, complete with braids and sprayed-on sparkles, and turned it into a Freddy Krueger-style nightmare with rabies and stake-hung cavalry. My bad!

I've certainly got my fair share of scars from the journey. But I've also got stories to tell. Moments to share. And two beautifully crazy children to remind me of the chaos when I'm old and unable to wipe... the soup from my chin *(see, I didn't go where you thought I was going to there!)*

I do sometimes wonder if the quality of their childhood will be reflected in the flavour of soup I end up with. I mean, I'm not a fan of tomato - that just feels a bit generic. And I'm allergic to mushrooms, so in theory, they could finish me off with one large spoonful.

Not a good way to go.

Cause of death: Mushroom-related asphyxiation.
Situation avoidable: Yes. By not feeding the deceased fungus.

It's not fatal-fatal. I usually just end up rolling around the floor in mild to moderate pain, clutching my stomach and re-evaluating my life choices. And honestly, I'd *hope* the number of people walking this earth who actively wish to inflict that kind of gastroenteritis-based punishment on me is a very short list.

But the thought sticks, doesn't it? That one day, someone else will hold the power. Over your comfort, your dignity... even your soup.

A while back, I did jokingly mention to my daughter that when I'm old and in my final days, she'll be responsible for my every need. I told her there would be no shoving me into some budget-friendly care home with peeling wallpaper and custard that tastes like regret. And definitely no abandoning me in some not-so-local café, where strangers take turns to balance teaspoons on my head while I nod off in a floral armchair.

Oh no. She must take me in, cook me meals, wash my pants with love, and whisper sweet nothings into my ear like, *"Mum, the cat didn't pee on your slippers today."*

But much to my horror, this heartfelt arrangement was met with her somewhat standard eye roll delivery, a sarcastic *"Uh-huh,"* and some half-baked excuse about there being no room in the vintage camper van she's planning to live in. Apparently, it's already occupied by a rescue dog, a compost toilet, and her need for personal and crochet space.

So yeah… that was a no. A *not-a-chance, I've moved pitch, the dog bites, I'm now a vegan, you'd ruin the vibe* kind of no.

And honestly? I found it absolutely hilarious. She's me. Down to the feral energy and misplaced confidence. And if anyone deserves to leave me hanging in my twilight years while crocheting pot holders in the Highlands, it's her.

My son, on the other hand, I worry for him.

I worry who will be there when I'm, you know, not. He may only be eight at the time of typing out this book (*21st of February 2025 in case you were wondering*) and I'm certainly not writing him off - I happen to think he's going to be amazing, one way or another. But I'm also realistic. I know that his merry-go-round will probably spin faster than he's ready for. That the highs will feel like soaring, dizzying, and brilliant. And the lows might hit like a drop with no warning.

That in itself feeds my Mum guilt. And I know a lot of parents, and especially ASN parents, feel the same.

So what's the solution? What's the peace of mind, the mental and emotional green button of *'stick that in your coffee and down it'* that brings hope, and joy, and promise to all of mankind?

Yeah… there isn't one. Or, at least not beyond giving our kids every heartbeat of love and encouragement we've got, to help them find their feet in a world that's anything but steady.

And sometimes, that means pushing them through the really ugly dirt that life *(and seemingly me, with maths books)* throws at them.

It's an uncomfortable situation for us both, my son and me. All I want to do is wrap him up in an array of textured blankets and hide beneath some Amazon box-built fort. I want to take snacks *(some of which he hates, because otherwise I'm not getting any!)* and the TV remote so we can peek through a cardboard flap to watch funny cat videos.

And we do. But not all the time, because real life doesn't exist inside an Amazon box.

OK, that point is arguable! I mean, some of my best life-saving purchases have come from Amazon. Like my son's '*happy shoes*' – they stock the *only* brand and fit that truly work for him. Or the catnip spray that's infinitely better than finding seeds scattered throughout the house.

Then there was the *84-pack of cat yoghurt treats*. Noise-cancelling headphones for when Mama needs to work but the house is on full volume. Nanobeads for my hair extensions (which were great, until two weeks later when I impulsively got rid of my hair extensions… again), micro-nano toothbrushes – awesome for sensory overload gums.

Oh, and let's not forget my daughter's *extra-loud ding-a-ling-ling alarm clock*, which successfully wakes the neighbours three doors down while she, not eight inches away, passively evades the need to rise from the undead.

Anyone else struggle with that one? Anyone else want to raid their kid's bedroom, water gun in hand and megaphone in the other? No? Oh, ok.

I was thinking, if I could go back thirteen years, to when I was pregnant with my daughter and give *me* some advice, I'd probably start with something like,

"Quit thinking you're prepared for this - you're not. You can't be. It doesn't matter how many books you've read, or how many Mama-in-the-know get-togethers you've begrudgingly sat through - this symphony is about to get real. And you, my dear, are less 'conductor' and more 'after-show cleanup crew'. Now grab a bucket!"

Twelve years and nine months later, and guess who's still mopping up after said daughter? Oh yeah, that'll be me.

She undoubtedly has me wrapped around her pinky finger. Master of one hundred excuses. Queen of *"Just one more minute, Mum."* And honestly? I wouldn't change a thing.

But if I'm handing out hypothetical advice to my younger self, why stop there? After all, parenting isn't a *one-and-done* kind of lesson - it's a rollercoaster that loves to throw in extra loops (*or an extra child in my case)* just when you think you've nailed it.

And with that in mind, if I could go back to the day before my son was born, that conversation would probably start with,

"Ok, you might actually be crazy! All that home birth, mantra-chanting, zen-mama nonsense might feel like the perfect, peaceful way to welcome your son into the world. But, lady, buckle up - this kid is about to Twister through the next eighteen to forty-eight years of your life, and you'll be left mentally flying like that poor cow we all saw in the movie. You think your daughter's been a journey so far? Try taking this one in a clapped-out old Mustang, stacked with seventeen 'must-have' teddies, no aircon, an itchy foot glued to the gas pedal, no seatbelt, and nothing but Oreo biscuits to survive on. This - this is going to be something else. But this kid will love you to the ends of the earth. Hold on to that, no matter how tough it gets."

And I do. I hold onto that kid and squeeze him until he giggles, or burps in my face… which is not unheard of! I cuddle him at every opportunity, snuggle right down in the corner of the sofa, and lap up his attention like some scruffy Irish Wolfhound who's just been sprung from the rescue centre.

And do you know what? I don't feel even a tinge of Mum guilt for it.

Sure, I make a lot of mistakes. I screw up often. And even go to bed at night, annoyed at myself for missing the mark. But those kids? They never hold it against me. Not on my worst days. Not when I stumble, fumble, or flat-out fail. And that's something *pretty damn special.*

I won't take all the credit - they are their own people, with kind souls and hearts so much bigger than mine. But I'll let myself feel a little proud. Because I had a hand in that. I helped them get here.

And honestly? I couldn't be prouder.

A random performance is going on in the background as I wrap up this chapter – my son is playing 'Remember Me' on the piano downstairs, you know, the one from the movie, Coco.

He chose it for his exam, because he knows it's one of my favourites.

And I just love the way he plays it.

Notes From the Edge

10th February 2025 ♡

Frankie
The Orange Flavoured Moron!

I can't think straight today. I'm mentally and emotionally *done* from the weekend. And as my thoughts try to surface, *as I try to do something even partially productive*, I feel like I'm drowning in a pool of self-pity...

I'm just *tired.*

And *probably* being melodramatic, again... But this weekend was tough. And the aftermath? Still very much lingering in some heavy, unexplainable way.

Right now, I've got my headphones on, with some weird meditation music humming in my ears. And the cats are hovering in their tree tower thing, throwing me desperate '*feed us or we shall riot*' stares.

(25 minutes later...)
Ok, let's try this again... ˋ°•*⁀➷

The new boxercise machine (my latest get-fit craze) is a *massive* win. 2,000 hits later, and I can *barely* lift my arms. But at least I've punched the doom and gloom out of my system. No more self-pity gushing onto the page.

The *calming ocean sounds* have, in that time frame, been replaced by an *unexpectedly upbeat* track from the *Blues Brothers,* courtesy of my son from across the hallway.

And I can't help but smile.

It's funny how music can *completely* shift your mindset. I don't think I ever really noticed it until my boy found his own beat a few years ago.

Sure, I sang nursery rhymes to him, and we'd bop along to tunes in the car. But for him, music isn't just *background noise.* It *runs* through him, like blood to me, or Lambrini to *certain people.*

↳----➤ (You *know* who you are. You *know* that bottle of booze was the making, or rather, the *ruining,* many a wild night! But anyway...)

Today was piano class. And after the tough weekend, the emotional rollercoaster... No, the emotional cesspool of what should have been our downtime, I wasn't feeling overly optimistic.

To help you understand my anti-optimism (which is a bit like an anti-climax, only with less disappointment), you need to picture a penguin. A sad little penguin clutching a single ice cube.

Now imagine his face when you tell him *that's it.* That tiny cube of ice is all that's left of the South Pole. And if he can't keep it from melting? There will be no more poles, south or dancing, to waddle his woo-ha upon.

Slightly off-track, but you get the idea. And more importantly, get how I felt this morning. Just a sad little penguin with the weight of the South Pole in my hands...

Cue a message to Mr D, our piano teacher, to warn him to batten down the hatches and prepare for a storm. My sheep show of a child is coming. And class is going to be a write-off!

But I didn't actually need to send out a warning. You see, Mr D is just awesome. A real hero of a tutor, who always tries his best to understand the mission (usually as that mission walks through the front door) and rejig any lesson plans without missing a metaphorical beat (albeit in mismatching socks today!)

After sacking off our initial music school for a lack of understanding over my son's needs, despite their initial reassurance that they could meet my son's needs, and then repeatedly letting me down, over my son's needs... Mr D. appeared in my Google search, like a beacon of hope. Or, more accurately, like a rogue ukulele player at a death metal concert, refusing to back down.

And 18 months later, he's still plugging away at what he believes will be his prodigy... kind of. He has high hopes for my son. Big dreams. And a shed load of patience that I can only admire from the sofa afar...

Oh, Mr D. You are, if nothing else, gloriously optimistic. And me? I'm just hoping for a session where we get through three 'mistakes' without needing a live exorcism! But anyway.

Did my child enter the realms of Mozart, Beethoven, or Elton John today? No. No, he did not. But neither did he self-combust under any unnecessary pressures and expectations. Because there were none (thanks to Mr D's expert class rejig skills).

And that's pretty much how I'm winging our current state of affairs. I guess we don't always have to achieve anything more than getting by. I wrote about that in the first chapter, Survival. And I'm now thinking I should probably print, stick, and highlight sections of it on my office wall.

But that doesn't mean I'm not absolutely fried from trying. Forget penguins – I'm that egg that's been sat in the blistering hot pan for too long. The one that was forgotten by the chef, when some numpty in the canteen decided to go vegan mid-order.

Why, oh why, do we put so much pressure on ourselves? Like weary villagers spinning endless gold from straw, convinced that if we just work a little harder, a little longer, we'll finally be enough!

coughs, trips over own thoughts, pretends it was all intentional Where were we? Oh yes. Mourning a society that sets us up, like kindling around a fire of pressure.

From the minute we're born, we are under telescopic scrutiny to hit milestones and pole-vault mountains. I remember my daughter, now 12, being dragged through the 3-year check-up with a rather intimidating Health Visitor. And more so, the big cross that came when she couldn't walk the imaginary high wire, aka a skipping rope laid out on the ground.

'Your daughter appears to struggle with this. It looks like a development issue – we'll need to monitor the situation over the next 3-6 months with a view to refer her if no improvement is seen...'

Or, and hear me out here – maybe, just maybe, I hadn't thought to teach my preschooler this completely useless party trick?

I mean, forgive me for prioritising things like *basic survival* over training her for the circus. But sure, let's set up a *formal review process* for her inability to tightrope-walk across my living room rug.

Sounds reasonable...

Not!

Urgh! Can you feel my ever-so-slight animosity towards the 'system' that does, quite often, work against rather than with the people trapped within it? Can you? CAN YOU feel the sizzle as my temperature rises, like a jacket spud in the oven? One that's drowning in butter, smothered in beans, and topped with an unrestrainable amount of cheddar cheese!

There's a growing amount of food analogies going on here! I feel hunger may be part of the problem ☕

But today wasn't all bad. Given that I lost two of my son's 'safe' foods over the weekend, (one of which he decorated my kitchen floor with), and struggled to keep him from swinging off his shiny pendulum (a metaphor for his exacerbating mood swings rather than an actual swinging object in my living room), I'd say today has been... better.

Let me break down

➔ He got up in a semi-decent mood ✓
➔ Survived breakfast with his sister ✓ (although that almost went Pete tong when his favourite plate was stacked UNDER the bowls. He claimed it's made from 'flimsy' plastic. It is not)
➔ Played piano for at least 7 minutes of his 30-minute lesson ✓

- ➔ Ate lunch. And liked the homemade doughnuts, despite having to wait an extra 34 minutes for them to cook and cool, meaning they were no longer connected to the lunchtime shindig ✓ ✓
- ➔ We avoided any and all stress, carnage, and crisis points that could have easily fallen into the cracks of our afternoon ✓

And honestly, I'll take all of those things, shake them up and down, and watch them sparkle, like the most beautiful snow globe in the world. Not because life is perfect – far from it. But because even in the mess, the glitter still flies if you're willing to shake it hard enough ♡

"There are going to be good days and bad days...
and you have to learn to fight through that." – Zach LaVine

Chapter 6: Balls To That

Because waiting your turn is a scam...
And he knows it.

I did promise at the start of this book some *potentially* helpful suggestions... ideas... I don't know. *Stuff that works for us.* And this chapter holds my first '*Grand Gesture'* in that department.

I mean, we've had some laughs, some tears, and shared some mental images that you'll *never* be able to erase *(here's to many more of those!)* But now, I want to take you back to 2019, to before our diagnosis journey began. Back to a time before labels, before clinical waiting rooms, before hours of paperwork that sapped the life from my soul.

Back to when I was just trying to survive life with a three and seven year old.

Now, if you've ever met, lived with, or given birth to something that later became a three-year-old *(because giving birth to an actual three-year-old is an eye-watering 'Don't you dare come near me with that weapon of mass destruction' thought!)*, you'll know that patience is not their virtue.

For the most part, they are *ticking time bombs*, primed and ready to explode. And the only way to safely cut the red… no, yellow… *no, definitely red* wire, is to stand back and let them unleash their verbal thunderbolt.

"Mama, I need…"
"Mama, I want…"
"Mama, my leg is going to fall off…"

And, in many ways, my child was no different. His outbursts were just as relentless as any other kid's. Just as high-pitching and last-nerve pinching. And delivered with the kind of dramatic flair that would make a Jeremy Kyle guest pause mid-chair throw.

The difference? His words were fuelled by echolalia - a term we'd never even heard of, until a Speech and Language Therapist casually dropped it into his records at four and a half. Like it was a standard Tuesday thing. Just a casual *"Oh, by the way, he repeats things a lot because of a neurological language processing difference"*, and then carried on like she'd just commented on the weather.

Sorry, what now?!
Repeats things?
Like… on purpose?
For fun?
For trauma?
Is this a problem?
Should I be doing something?
Buying something?
Calling someone?

His words would fire out on repeat, like salted popcorn exploding in an unattended microwave - violent, chaotic, and somehow burning itself into the ceiling. Or worse, like Dill Pickle-flavoured corn, assaulting the air with the kind of betrayal you can't ever fully scrub out.

"A B C… A B C… A B C… A B C… C… C…."
"Da Mama love me? Da Mama love me? Yes? Yes? Da Mama love me? Yes?"
"It's blue. Da bus is blue. Blue bus. Blue bus. Da bus is blue…"

And taking turns in conversation? Not happening. The idea that *"Mama's just on the phone"* or *"Mama would really like to pee in peace - give me 30 seconds"* was completely lost on him. If he had something to say, it needed to be said. And right now.

I tried so hard to break through, to show him that waiting was just as important as talking. But with his limited understanding, it was like shouting instructions into a storm.

If I said *"Shhh,"* he'd go *"Shh, shh, shh."*
If I said *"Hang on,"* he'd gleefully parrot back *"Hang on!"*

And if I tried to ignore it? Yeah. That did sweet fig all. He just kept going, happily babbling away like a one-man radio station.

I'm not gonna lie - those months were brutal. *(Thirty-seven of them, but it felt more like fifty-seven, measured in sleepless nights and slowly fraying patience!)* I loved his little voice, so sweet, so happy. He was, and still is, the kind of kid whose rainbows always come out to play. Whose smile could light up a room, like a scene from a movie.

But it was bittersweet, because behind all that sunshine was the constant, bone-deep exhaustion I couldn't escape. The relentless noise. The endless repetition. The feeling that I was trying to build a house out of smoke, expecting it to make it stand, while everyone else clapped like it was easy.

Was I warned this would be my life? Absolutely.

"Sleep while you can," they said. *"Because once that baby arrives, you'll be lucky to pee without an audience and your dinner will always be cold. Welcome to parenthood, sweetheart."*

Awesome. Only my son wasn't my first DNA drop, so I'd already been inducted into that sacred *"I solemnly swear to screw up my parents in the most loving, snot-covered, 3am-tantrum, first-word-then-fart-noise, snuggle-bunny, what's-that-smell?"* oath they all seem to arrive with.

I knew the drill. I'd done the stamping tantrums, the green vegetable refusal, the relentless questions. And I had, in fact, already made peace with the sleep-deprived shenanigans, along with the fact that my brain officially ceased to function somewhere between the fifth and seventh week of sleep training... *the first time around!*

But my son was, is, different. My exhaustion with him didn't come from sleepless nights or relentless outbursts. No, it came from... comes from, trying my absolute best to listen, all day long, as he echoes random YouTube facts, or narrates his latest tablet gameplay. It comes from being his go-to. His safe place, even when I'm in the bathroom and he's rambling through the door. It comes from being his partner in periodic tables, the eight times table, and his *"What's for dinner"* on the table.

Am I lapping it up like the last puppy at the pet shop, where the wee girl comes in and gives a tickle under the neck or a rub on the belly? Absolutely! But I'm only human, and as such, I needed to find a way to temporarily suspend the signal to the one-man radio... *(which in my head, looks something like the movie "The Boat That Rocked" - an awesome film if you haven't seen it!)*

Time for a not-so-random fact - that was one of the very few movies I've actually seen at the cinema. I've been with the kids a couple of times, but let's be real, it's just not the same.

They squirm. They talk. They drop popcorn in places no popcorn should ever be. They get bored *halfway through*, then suddenly find *urgent interest* in the film *right* as I'm sneaking a look at my phone to check how much longer I have to sit through it.

And without sounding old (*but absolutely sounding old*), *have you seen the prices these days?!* I could buy a *small island* for the cost of a large popcorn and a drink.

I really should go to the cinema for something less Minions-related. But as a parent, those 'fun' things definitely get brushed aside. My weekend outing now consists of a trip to ASDA, well, it did today at least, followed by a mad dash to launch everything into the freezer *before* it defrosts.

And if I *really* play my cards right? A sneaky escape to the office with some anti-diet food and an irresponsibly large cup of coffee.

I probably won't actually go to the cinema. Netflix, Amazon Prime and iPlayer have enough terrible movies. And more importantly, no one here judges me for watching them in my oddie covered in snack crumbs, like a feral woodland creature.

Times have changed! But anyway...

After an unhealthy amount of online research *(the kind you end up doing after a specialist throws a ton of fancy terms at you and you nod like you understand)*, the long-awaited penny finally dropped. Things started to make more sense.

It turns out that echoing words and phrases, the thing that was driving me half mad, is actually a normal part of childhood development. At least, according to Dr Google *(who, side note, should never be trusted with real emergencies or to self-diagnose an itchy ear. After all, everything is fatal if you believe the internet. Even shampoo irritation. Not that I've ever done that, obviously!)*

Apparently, this whole copy-and-paste communication system usually lasts until around three years old. It is how kids learn language *(including all the words you hope they would not, like that accidental F-bomb you dropped when you stubbed your toe).*

In their own sweet time *(much like with everything else)*, our little record-and-play megaphones develop their own repertoire, complete with inappropriate monologues with snippets from anywhere and everywhere. And before you know it, you have a walking-talking exhibit of all your parenting screw-ups to date!

Isn't that fun?!

Of course, these outbursts have to be delivered the second they spring to mind. And interrupting conversations to do so is part and parcel of their little worlds, until around seven years old.

Seven years? Seven years of *"Just a minute"* or *"I'm in the middle of a conversation, can it wait?"*

Fudge me with a greased-up watermelon! I did not agree to that at the time of conception. No one invited me to read the small print. Or recite the terms and conditions prior to the point of no return!

Of course, I'm joking... mostly!

Yes, those child-related parenting gripes will lessen with gentle persuasion and improper humour - my longstanding retort has always been, *"If you don't stop, I'm gonna rip your arm off and slap you with the soggy end..."* which is effective, as they're 99.8% sure that I'm joking, and yet not willing to push me and find out for certain!

Still, seven years is a whole lot of butting in on conversations.

And if you're going to throw Autism and/or ADHD into the mix, well, you'd likely get less time in prison for drug trafficking... *(Not that I'm suggesting you jump free with a ten-year break, of course - it's just good to know these things!)*

So, why is waiting *so* much harder for our spectrum kiddos?

Well, for one, it's not always about understanding how to wait - it's understanding *why* they're being asked to wait in the first place. The words make sense, the instructions are clear, but the *actual* act of putting it into practice? That's where it falls apart.

Much like my ability to 'Keep Calm' when comforted with an ink-a-phobe on a sunny Friday afternoon, while wearing a vest top and showing off my tattooed.. I mean mutilated, skin like some poster girl for the Hep B vaccine...

At four, five, and even six years old, my son wasn't missing social cues - he hadn't even reached the point where they *existed* for him yet. The idea that someone else might be talking, that a conversation even has a rhythm or a natural pause to jump into, just wasn't on his radar.

"But what if I forget what I need to say?" became a knee-jerk reaction. And even the *mere* thought of waiting, ping-ponging around in his head, became completely overwhelming.

That wasn't just a kid struggling with patience. That was a brain wired differently - one that doesn't play by standard rules, no matter how nicely you ask.

Because my son doesn't come with a standard settings menu. No, he's running the full double feature of Autism and ADHD. It's the ultimate tug of war: one part of his brain craves order, familiarity, and structure, while the other is launching thought-rockets into space without warning. Mid-sentence, mid-meal, mid pull-up change...

And it's gone. Blasted off like a cosmic fact cannon.

Me, however? I've got my own ADHD party going on upstairs, with an internal cheerleader squad, jacked up on energy drinks, yelling, *"SAY IT! SAY IT NOW OR YOU'LL NEVER REMEMBER IT AGAIN!"*

There's no queue.
No holding pattern.
Just a rogue thought, seven more in hot pursuit, and a brain like a leaky sieve made of smoke.

Let's be honest - my logic and impulse control do *exist*, technically. But most of the time, they're lying face down in the gutter while my mouth takes over, megaphone in hand, already halfway through the punchline.

You laugh. I laugh. But yet, it's painfully accurate.

Another Small Disclaimer:

Before anyone jumps on my case with a *"Don't lump all neurodivergent people into one box - that's not fair!"* speech, don't worry. I'm not. I know everyone's experience is different. Autism and ADHD are incredibly diverse, and there's no single roadmap that fits us all.

I'm simply sharing our reality - the things that have challenged us, the things that have helped, and the things that still leave me, a middle-aged woman with undiagnosed ADHD *(the same ADHD that's been quietly gate-crashing my life for decades, and probably the only reason this book even exists thanks to a hyper-fixation episode),* scratching my head at 2am, wondering if I've done the right thing.

And with my son's brain flitting between the beautiful chaos of Autism and ADHD, when I talk about the internal push-pull, the noise, the overwhelm, the impulse to blurt while simultaneously trying not to forget your own name… I'm not just saying it for attention.

I'm saying it because it's real.
And believe it or not, I'm not here to upset anyone.

Although, to be fair, I'm pretty sure I've written something in this book to offend just about everyone if you squint at it the right way.

And honestly, if you've made it this far and only just decided to be outraged, high-five. Your stamina is genuinely impressive.

The part that really makes me smile? It's usually the same people, the ones who are horrified by a devil's tea party joke or a harmless jab at vegan oat-shakes... That fall about laughing at my son's explosive bathroom commentary, or my casual mentions of hookers and drugs (so to speak).

Yes, I might be inappropriate. I might cross the line. But let's be real – you probably laughed at something equally offensive ten pages ago. And if not? Stick around. You probably will in ten pages from now.

Honestly, it's your choice. You can live and let live, laugh when you know you probably shouldn't, and breathe a little lighter. Or, you know, hate the world, throw me into the middle of it like a human dartboard, and scream into the void.

Whatever helps you sleep at night. That's free will.

And honestly? I think we're pretty damn lucky to have that.

Now, circling back to the whole *'please stop interrupting'* saga - I did eventually find a better way to explain to my now slightly more together eight-year-old, that waiting to speak is OK.

That the sky will not fall down.
The nation's cheese supply will remain un-doused in fizzy cola *(aka his favourite food, ruined by his least favourite)*.
And his mouth will *not* be zipped shut for all eternity, just because he had to metaphorically gag his innermost thoughts for a few extra moments.

Sounds like parenting magic, right? Like I've cracked the code to conversational bliss. But before I share all, there's one thing you need to know:

There. Is. No. Secret. Code.

No one-size-fits-all.
No magic phrase that instantly makes them zip it.
No *"Look over there!"* distraction that actually works beyond the age of three.
No government-issued manual titled *'How to Get Five Minutes of Peace Without Offering Your Soul as Payment.'*
No legal way to temporarily rehome your child when they start narrating your private phone calls in real-time.

There just isn't.

Urgh! Balls to that!

Yes, *balls*, as in my epically named '*Ball of Conversation'* concept.

Do you like what I did there? No? Yeah, me neither.

It wasn't exactly the *seamless* switchover I was going for, but honestly, there's no *graceful* way to swerve from *scandalous joyriding* straight into *deeply profound parenting wisdom.*

You can take that cheesy transition as a bleak reminder, though, that I am but a sleep-deprived Mama bear with only enough coffee to come up with one outstanding idea a day.

And I'm big enough to admit that that awful punchline was not it... Sorry!

Shall we move on?
Yeah, I think so.

Chapter 7: Still Got Balls

Our DIY guide to conversation skills
(No Pinterest boards required!)

OK, I lied. Sort of.

I told you Chapter 4 would be my first *'Grand Gesture'* in potentially helpful suggestions… and instead, you got long-winded tangents about echolalia, YouTube parroting, parenting exhaustion, and ADHD chaos.

Insightful? Maybe.
Straight to the point? Absolutely not.

But this chapter *is* the real deal. The *'Here's what actually worked for us'* section. The part where I pretend to have my life together, just long enough to explain a method that didn't involve bribery, begging, or hiding in the bathroom with a packet of chocolate digestives *(although they are all valid options, should you so wish to use them!)*

Now, if you're hoping for one of those neat, step-by-step parenting guides filled with calm suggestions and gentle affirmations… You may want to lower your expectations.

Like really lower them, down to the underworld, past the motivational demons and Karens of the earth, until those 'expectations' are doing shots with Lucifer and asking him if this counts as a parenting workshop.

But if you're up for a messy, honest, and heartfelt breakdown of how I taught my interrupt-prone son the basics of conversation turn-taking, then pull up a chair. You're in the right place.

We didn't start with flashcards or Pinterest-perfect social scripts. Oh no. We started with a ball. A real, actual ball. Not metaphorical. Not parenting-blog certified. Just a thing you throw, and, if you're lucky, catch again.

It wasn't shiny or squishy or full of *'knock knock'* jokes *(although that would have been kind of cool!)* It was just something simple. Something he could hold in his hands.

And it turned out that's exactly what my kid needed.

As you've already heard or read, we were having so many issues with taking turns in conversation, especially when it came to listening. Not because he was being rude or difficult, but because he genuinely didn't understand how conversations worked.

The back and forth.
The natural pause.
The rhythm of give and take… it just didn't click.

So this ball? It gave us both something we *could* click with.

We started by sitting on the floor and rolling the ball between us. The person holding the ball was the one talking. The other person listened. That was the rule.

It sounds almost too simple to work, but that's what made it effective. There was a physical marker for whose turn it was. No guessing. No confusion. Just a small, gentle prompt to help him practise the art of waiting.

And at first, I had to guide him with, *"OK, time to roll it back now",* otherwise, he would have happily chatted on for hours while I slowly lost all feeling in my legs on the laminate floor. But slowly, he started to get it. That pause, that moment of, *"Oh, I've had my turn,"* started landing.

Next, I asked his big sister to come play our conversation game. When it was my son's turn to pass the ball, both my daughter and I called out, *"To me! To me!"* at the same time. And suddenly, he had a decision to make.

Who should he pass it to?
Whose turn was it to talk?

It caught him off guard. But it also gave him a small insight into how it feels when *everyone* wants to speak at once. It threw off the flow, which he didn't like. But that discomfort? That *was* the lesson.

Next, I introduced a second ball with a different topic. Both were rolled towards him at the same time. And again, he got frustrated. The noise, the split focus, the pressure to respond… It was too much. And again, *that* was the point.

Not because I want him to struggle - never that. But because I know he learns best through experience, not lectures. And sometimes, the most powerful way to teach understanding is to let him feel what it's like when no one's listening to him either.

Because, to me, that's how you build real awareness. Not from being told *"You need to wait your turn,"* but from experiencing what it's like when someone else doesn't.

And weirdly enough, it worked. Our little blue ball turned into an anchor - a way to make conversations feel real, something solid in a world that often felt anything but. It didn't fix everything overnight, but it cracked the door open. And sometimes, that's enough.

Now, if he jumps into a conversation mid-topic, I'll say, *"Is this your ball of conversation?"* And more often than not *(unless it's a deal breaker in his eyes)*, he'll stop, smile a little, and say, *"No, it's not."*

Sometimes, he'll even ask, *"Is this a good time to start a new topic?"*

like a tiny diplomat checking the room, which makes me beam with pride.

And when it is his turn? I always give him my full attention.

Because if he's working hard to wait, then I want him to know that waiting doesn't mean being ignored. It means being heard properly when the moment comes.

✦✦✦ *Devil's Advocate Reviews* ✦✦✦
Legitimacy Sold Separately

"Before Lucifer's Parenting Workshops, I thought raising kids was about love, patience, and gentle guidance. Now I know it's mostly about snacks, sarcasm, and strategic hiding. Five stars. Would sell my soul again." - A Very Tired Mum.
★★★★★

"Lucifer's Parenting Workshops taught me that 'fake it till you make it' is a totally valid strategy. Also that nobody actually knows what they're doing. Especially me." - Dave, Father of Three,
Surviving on Caffeine and Regret
★★★★★

Chapter 8: Stuck on Repeat

Like a Broken Record,
But Funnier.

What's that one phrase you hear yourself saying over, and over, and over again?

"Stop licking the dog - I know where it's been!"
"What do you mean you forgot to put pants on?"
"No, the cat does not want your cheese sandwiches."
"I haven't had enough coffee to deal with this yet!"

For me, it's definitely the latter. And given that I've been roaming practically caffeine-free of late *(a mere three to four cups a day, in contrast to my regular eight to ten),* the world is feeling that much tougher to face at times.

Thank goodness my son is on the ball, though. He is relentlessly charging through, and high on spirit, albeit somewhat low on empathy for my tiredness.

Oh, child-encrusted empathy, where did you go? At times, you rush in like an overconfident tourist in a revolving door. But now, now you mock me, like the top-shelf biscuits that I just can't quite reach.

Eww. I just made it sound like my child has some crusty disease. As though he flakes upon every surface, and sprinkles like a leper in a wind tunnel. Ha! My bad.

And he doesn't, just so you know! I wanted to make that bit crystal clear.

This isn't exactly off to a great start, which is mildly concerning given we're barely a page into the chapter! Truth be told, I rarely plan out these epilogues. There's no grand writer's vision, no giant whiteboard covered in complex diagrams and colour-coded post-its. That being said, I do send myself the occasional WhatsApp message, with "Things I should add!" And today's gem? A reminder of how my daughter declared, "Cauliflower looks like a broccoli that didn't make it." Her outlook on life is... unique, to say the least.

I do also have points I want to cover, topics I've loosely stitched together. I've salvaged some of the better bits from the first draft (a version that was never meant to be because, frankly, it was drab, soulless, and read like it was written by a PTA committee... Hard to believe I know, but it is what it is!) And the rest? Well, that just sort of happens. Life happens. And I write about it.

We're very, *very* used to repetition in this house. As I've mentioned a few times now *(you know, like a broken record)*, my son has echolalia, aka human parrot episodes.

> *Around 75% of autistic individuals experience echolalia at some stage in their development.*

This involuntary echoing of words and phrases can happen immediately, like when I shouted, *"Frankie just slam dunked the wall!"* which, for the record, resulted in ten straight minutes of rhythmic repetition and uncontrollable laughter… My bad. Again!

Other times, the echoes arrive much later, often courtesy of YouTube reruns, with every tiny detail flawlessly mimicked, tone, accent, and all.

It's part of how my son communicates, and I love that about him. But sometimes, he gets stuck in a loop. And I don't mean a gentle *"oops, wrong turn"* kind of loop. No, I mean *a full-throttle, hamster-on-a-caffeine-binge stuck in a wheel, lost in an IKEA showroom with no exit signs, tangled up in a plate of overcooked spaghetti and don't forget the marinara sauce* kind of loop.

That can be frustrating for him and us, and so I developed...

Ha! A helpful bit. I completely forgot to pre-highlight this with an 'Upcoming Performance!' announcement - oops. No flashing lights, no dramatic drumroll. Just me, throwing it at you like an unmarked tin from the back of the cupboard... Surprise!

But for the record, this bit might actually be useful. You know, just in case you came here for *helpful* content rather than an extended commentary on my questionable life choices.

Looping*, as we call it, is when my son gets stuck on an endless verbal treadmill. It happens when he's trying to form his own sentence, but just can't seem to reach the finish line, as if his brain knows exactly what it wants to say, but somewhere between thought and speech, the signal glitches. And so instead of carrying on, he hits restart, again and again. Sometimes from the beginning, sometimes halfway through. But always a restart.

*(Quick Note: *Looping isn't an official clinical term - it's just the word we use to describe when my son gets stuck emotionally on a thought, a worry, or a phrase. It's different from echolalia, which is about repeating words for communication or language development. Looping, on the other hand, is about emotional processing - when something feels too overwhelming to move past easily.)*

And honestly, once you've seen it, you can't unsee it. Looping can look like stubbornness or distraction on the outside, but underneath, it's just his brain trying its hardest to untangle a knot that doesn't want to loosen.

As his Mum, I always want to rush in and help. I want to say, *"It's OK, forget it,"* or just finish the sentence for him, to save him the struggle. But I know, deep down, that's not what he needs.

So instead, I suggested gently pointing it out when he was looping. Not in a *"gotcha"* kind of way. The last thing I want is for him to feel like he's doing something wrong. But rather, an acknowledgement, a mental nudge, to help break the cycle.

Now, all I say is, *"Looping."*
That's it.

And he'll either say *"OK"* to me, or *"Stop"* to himself. And somehow, it works.

He's not frustrated that I interrupt him, or pent up because he doesn't get to finish whatever he's trying to say. He just gets it and moves on, with almost a sigh of relief that he's been given that grace.

For a while, he did try saying sorry. Every time, a small, automatic apology. And, understandably, I had to stop him. I had to step in. Because it wasn't his fault, and he shouldn't grow up thinking it ever was.

Honestly, that's something I'm determined to protect. I don't want my kids feeling like they have to excuse who they are. I don't want them to feel shame or hide away because of their differences or their struggles.

I did it for a long time, hiding the darkness from those who didn't want to see it, turning up and putting on the *'Good Girl Show'*, just to be accepted. But the truth? I never really was.

For me, growing up felt like wearing a pair of shoes that almost fit - close enough to walk in, but never without discomfort. I carried extra weight, physically, yes, but also in the way I didn't *really* feel like I belonged. The half-sibling in a family of full-blood ties made me easy to single out. And I was forever left feeling like an afterthought in my own childhood, in my own home.

School was equally a living nightmare. I was the easy target - different enough to be mocked but not quite odd enough to be cast out completely. I was the entertainment, an emotional punch bag, disguised as a friend. And although I didn't know it then, ADHD, laced with social anxiety, played a huge part in that. I was desperate to be liked, to be accepted, to not feel like I was floating alone.

At sixteen, I'd had enough - enough of feeling like I was merely tolerated rather than wanted, like I was always on the outside looking in. So I left. I figured if my family and so-called friends were never really going to see me, then I'd go where I couldn't be overlooked. I'd find people who had no choice but to notice me, even if it meant going to extremes to make that happen.

I quickly fell into a world where attention was currency. Modelling, dancing, drinking, playing the part of someone confident, someone exciting… Someone people actually wanted to be around.

I craved validation like oxygen, but ultimately, I drowned in it.

I went over the top, said yes when I should have said no, drank when I should have walked away. I let people define me because I didn't know how to define myself.

And in the end? I was still just as lonely.

It took years to untangle that mess, to step away from the need for external approval and sit comfortably in who I actually am. And it's only in the last five or six years that I've started seeing myself as someone worth accepting, not because of what I do for others, but because I am a good person.

Now, as a mother, I carry that weight differently. I don't want my kids to feel what I felt, to believe that their worth is dictated by other people's opinions. I know I can't shield them from it all. But I can make damn sure that they know exactly who they are, and that they never need to change to fit someone else's version of *'acceptable.'*

Tonight, just before bed *(because obviously that's when all vital life questions surface),* my son asked, "Mum, how does the washing machine know how to wash different clothes on the mixed cycle?"

I explained something about cotton blends and machine logic, but he wasn't buying it.

"So basically, you just can't be bothered to wait for the proper cotton cycle?" he said, like a tiny prosecutor catching me out.

Cornered, I compared it to his Cherries 'n Berries juice being better than the other options - not necessary, just preferred.

Apparently, that was enough. Case closed. Bedtime delayed by another twenty minutes.

When my brain isn't already deep-fried, I like to refresh my coffee-to-blood ratio and invite my emotionally charged ostrich in for a *talk.* And by *talk,* I mean him talking *at* me, either about things I've already heard twenty times or topics so complex they fly straight over my head like a deranged pigeon on a sugar high.

His current obsession *(if I haven't mentioned it before… I honestly can't remember at this point)* is coding levels for *'Geometry Dash'.* In this game, he spends an *irresponsible-parenting* amount of time designing platforms, tweaking moves, and showcasing his self-taught coding skills.

It would be impressive...
No, it is impressive. However, I am honestly confused for 99.9% of it.

But isn't that how parents and children should be, though? Them, perpetually baffled by the endless *life lessons* we throw their way. The rules, the expectations, the relentless, and *apparently* unnecessary nagging.

And us, staring in bewilderment at how suddenly they grow up. How these tiny humans who once clapped along to *Old McDonald* are now ranting about the wrongs of slavery, debating how ethical carrot waffles are in the child vs vegetable war, or trying to explain in words that I don't even understand, why some guy on YouTube screaming at video games is a millionaire.

He's still so little, though, my son. Not in his jeans and trainers, but in his place within the world. It all feels so fragile, so uncertain.

And I'm just sat here, struggling to make sense of it all and figure out how best to guide him.

Because let's face it - parenting is hard, full stop. Whether our kids are neurotypical *(a word I loathe, by the way, like typical and ordinary are somehow acceptable ways to describe the next generation of beings)* or prinkled, or rather doused with a little extraness.

(And yes, I hear you - there is nothing extra about sleepless nights, suspicious stains on freshly painted walls, or seventeen consecutive dinner rejections. But I'm digging deep for the positives here!)

No, raising kids isn't just about surviving the daily madness. It's about helping them find their place in a world that won't always make room for them. And that? That's the part that knots my stomach at 2am.

I worry. Not in a *writing him off* kind of way, no, never. I have zero doubts that my son will carve a beautiful path and be a hero in his own right. I can picture it now, up on stage, playing piano with the same passion that makes his fingers dance across the keys in our living room. Or at the very least, standing beside me, pointing out every marketing flaw in the sequel to the sequel of this book! The joys.

Yes, I know there *are* options for young people who need additional help. Halfway accommodations, supported living, gentle nudges into independence rather than a full-blown shove. And I'm sure when the time comes, we'll figure it out.

But I'd be lying if I said I wasn't scared. As I've grudgingly, and painfully, admitted more times than I'd like, the world isn't always kind. And as much as I want him to fly, to find his own way, I'm in no rush to watch him disappear into the world.

Besides, if he stays home forever, at least I'll always have someone to reach the top-shelf biscuits!

'Goodness gracious, Great Balls of Fire!'

That was today's echo of all echoes. You see, my emotionally charged ostrich has recently discovered the joys of '50s and '60s rock 'n' roll.

Chuck Berry has a lot to answer for from his grave.

Amd as for Jerry Lee Lewis? Well, he's practically an accomplice at this point.

Every time my boy shrieked the 'great' in *Great Balls of Fire* and then collapsed into laughter, it threw me into a heart-warming state of amusement. I had no idea why it was so funny, but his uncontrollable giggles were impossible to ignore, not that I'd want to, of course.

And without warning, I found myself laughing too, with tears streaming down my face. 'Happy tears', he calls them. "Mum, you've got happy tears."

As we pulled up home, our neighbours were privy to a complete 'balls of fire' dance-along performance. I clocked the usual curtain twitchers as we walked up the path, the side stares, and the pretence that they didn't hear us... just brilliant!

But do you know what? I don't care. He was happy. I was happy. And if Jerry Lee Lewis had been watching from the great beyond, I think even *he* would've cracked a grin.

"Who stole my chicken burrito? I was saving that!"
"Where's the thing? The TV channel-changing thing? Huh? What do you mean I just need to wave my hand and shout 'funny cat videos'?"
"I could have sworn I made a cuppa... Oh well, I'll make another. Hold on - who keeps leaving mugs to go cold on the counter?!"

These are just some of the things I'm sure I'll say on repeat when I'm an elderly warthog, shuffling around in slippers two sizes too big, talking to inanimate objects and driving everyone within a ten-metre radius absolutely bananas.

I'll grunt at cushions, argue with the microwave, and demand answers from the poor unsuspecting lamp that, in my fading eyesight, looks suspiciously like my daughter ignoring me.

And when everyone groans and rolls their eyes, I'll smile, knowing that karma, poetic justice, revenge… whatever you want to call it… came knocking eventually.

After years of patiently *(and sometimes not-so-patiently)* decoding my son's loops and echolalic echoes, the tables will have turned. It'll be him, rubbing his temples, muttering, *"Mum, you already told me. Five times."*

And honestly?
I'll just be there, smiling into my lukewarm tea, thinking… *worth it!*

Notes From the Edge

17th February 2025 ♡

I don't care what sweet Mary Poppins facelift you're pulling off, what gentle parenting mantra you're preaching, or how many double vodka espressos you've slammed back this morning – there isn't a single parent alive who wants to be woken up to the sound of their child squealing on a Monday.

But that's what happened. And at that frightfully disoriented cat licking my face moment, I had no idea if it was squeals of excitement, fear, pain, or just life.

Yup, my kid is really good at that last one. As a stimmer, a ticker, a tapper, a bobadi booer, noises are part and parcel.

But forgive me for not being totally on board with this latest stimtastic moment, for my alarm was yet to scream at me, and so my day was not yet ready to start.

Stop the bus, I want to get off already! °+·—♡

Today is Monday. But today is NOT piano Monday. Mr D. is not in da house... Well, he's never in my house – that would be kind of weird. But then again, Monday without piano lesson is kind of weird.

We like our routines. Even us home edders, home workers, home coffee drinkers... yes, the world can be at times, too peopley... ers! Home solves that problem without the need for awkward niceties!

And when routine lets us down quicker than an ex dodging child support, I'm not so much rolling with it as praying to any religion that'll take me on a 24-hour trial period.

> ╰---➤ Incidentally, if you think I'm being rude about religion, you're absolutely right. But I've earned it. You see, I grew up in a Catholic household, where my mother hung a cross in the hallway... and her knickers out the window. (Sorry, Jesus!)
>
> Within our 4 walls, religion was more smoke screen than salvation. And 'Oh my God' was mostly chanted from the bedroom whenever Dave... no, Danny... or was it Derek? came to visit.
> (Honestly, at this point, even Jesus probably lost track.)

Oops – over-sharing seems to be a talent of mine! Probably my millennial mind overcompensating for the lack of people to confide in as a kid, because, well, my mother was too busy sharing with everyone else... Wow, that felt good! Monday's looking up already!

So why no piano lesson with the hero we call Mr D? Because it's half-term. A school half-term. A school thing. Even though we're not in school, and do not live by the 39 weeks of term, we are still sanctioned by the dreaded peak-time holidays.

Pluck a duck (sorry duck! 🦆)

Slight tangent – but I used to get *really* hung up on people saying, "Home ed is just an *excuse*. A lazy way out for parents who can't be bothered." Like we were all just lounging around in pyjamas, dodging responsibility and letting our kids grow up feral. It used to really get under my skin.

But here's the thing – once you actually look into how little focused learning time happens during an entire school day, the tables don't just turn. No, they flip. They do a jig. Then they do another flip, upside down, inside out, and reveal a big fat *"Stick that in your rule book and burn it"* drawing, etched into the bottom and outlined in glittery permanent marker.

Goldfish to represent the lack of brain cells bobbing
around in certain classrooms ⤶

🐟 🐟 🐟 🐟 🐟 🐟 🐟 🐟 🐟

Despite how it looks, I'm not anti-school. I think it's a fantastic correctional facility for many young people.

But humour me on this –

↳>> The average secondary school day: – 6.5 hours
>>> Minus 15-minute morning break + 1-hour lunch break (*because even prisoners get exercise*)

↳>> Lose another 10 minutes for *"register and rants"* first thing, another 10 after lunch, plus 10 more for *"packing up"* (*a process that somehow takes three times longer than unpacking*)
>>> Subtract: the 20-minute daily assembly, which is mostly spent practising religion and/or school conformity.

And then there's the actual lessons...

↳>> First 5 minutes: settling down, hunting for a missing pen, and some poor sod realizing they've been in the wrong classroom this whole time
>>> Last 5 minutes: aggressively shoving books into bags while the teacher yells, *"The bell doesn't dismiss you, I do!"*
↳>> At least 10 minutes per class: *brain break*, because nobody can endure algebra or Henry VIII's love life without zoning out for at least a little while
>>> Minimum 5 minutes per lesson: teacher vs. reprobates featuring classic hits like *"PUT YOUR CHAIR DOWN, JASON"* and *"Do I look like I care if your pen is broken?"*

So, that leaves us with... *drum roll...*

"Around 2 hours and 20 minutes of actual learning a day,
for 5 days a week, and 39 weeks per year!"

Only, that's assuming there are no teacher strike days, no sick days, no dental appointments that somehow take half a day, and no *"Sir, my Great Aunt Gertrude has died"* compassionate leave pleas, which can be anywhere between 1 and 8 days, depending on creative flair!

But home ed is failing our kids! Pluck a duck! (Sorry, duck, again! -,`🦆,´-)

Tangent over...

It's been OK today, surprisingly. I was a little concerned when my son echoed to me 27 times, "Today is not a Mr D day", but his self-regulation mantra seemed to work. And the semi-impromptu semi-planned visit to the yarn shop for a cuppa with the owner appeared to pass as a fair substitute.

Yes, I am talking about the right child here. Although my daughter is generally considered the crazy wiggle-wanderer, with her crochet and whatnot, my son is not adverse to the great balls of wool that fill this cosy shop. And the fact that he could take his cross stitch (yup, we're still going with it) made him feel included in the woolly event.

We've also had a *painfully* long discussion (well, I *tried* to discuss, but my boy was too busy launching into a full-scale rant) about why the post keeps arriving for the previous occupiers.

This did *not* make sense. It *broke* the rules of his world. We've lived here for over 2 years. That's more than 730 days (*yes, we counted*). So why, in his very logical mind, have these people *not* changed their address like *normal humans*? *WHY* is their mail *still* coming here?

He *hated* it. It *bothered* him. It was wrong. And the longer I failed to provide an acceptable answer, the *more* unacceptable the situation became.

Somewhere between *"Well, clearly, they're just irresponsible"* and *"What if MY post starts going to strangers?!"* (not that he actually gets post, but ya know), we ended up in a discussion about why some people *deliberately* don't update their address... Dodging bills. Avoiding payments. Being *shady*.

His verdict? "Well, that's just rude."

Agreed kid. Agreed. But there's not much I can do about it, other than keep sending it back to the companies.

Yes, there are definitely some conversations, some cans of worms, that I would rather not open with my smallest child. His 'logic' knows no variants, no letting go of the box marked 'The right way'. And I think that's going to be tough for him when he grows up.

Because life isn't always that black and white. Things don't always go perfectly to plan. And answers can't always be plucked from thin air... No matter how many frogs you kiss...

That aside, today is cake-baking day – the one place where I can confidently say my son will dive in with 2 freshly washed hands. He loves to bake with me. And after several months of feet stamping, he's now in a really good place with 'Close enough' on the scales.

300g of self-raising flour? 302 – close enough
220g of caster sugar? 223 – close enough
25 minutes in the oven? 26, because we got distracted... But that's close enough.

And honestly, I'm super proud of him for reaching that level of acceptance in at least this small part of his life ♡

> "*Change cannot be put on people. The best way to instill change is to do it with them. Create it with them.*" – Lisa Bodell

Chapter 9: Listening Ears

The struggle to be heard
(and heard properly).

What's that I hear? Is it *another somewhat useful* chapter? Surely not! Quick, alert the Parent Council - someone draft a passive-aggressive email and put the kettle on. This might actually qualify as *'constructive.'*

Oh, probably not.
Still, I got your attention, which is more than I can say for my kids of late.

Honestly, I am around 73% sure that the half-dead stem of broccoli in the bottom of the fridge has better listening skills than either of my children. Though now in a near-biohazard state, it gives me the silent treatment without pretending it's a personal protest.

Or maybe, just maybe, they *(the kids, not the cabbage)* are playing a blinder with their *'Fallen on Deaf Ears'* performance.

I mean, we're talking BAFTA Award-worthy acting- none of that B-rated movie nonsense in this house! The way they manage to completely omit my voice when asked to tidy their rooms or pick up their single sock from the bathroom floor is somewhat remarkable... *Infuriating,* but remarkable.

However, according to all the parenting books and self-proclaimed online gurus... You know, the ones who probably never had kids but earned a degree in *'Theoretical Parenting'* while sipping overpriced lattes... My children are doing exactly what they're meant to be doing.

They're being kids.

Yes, apparently, this selective hearing, along with an impressive ability to forget everything they were told within the last five seconds, are all signs of being a well-adjusted child.

Who knew? Not me, obviously! That's why I'm here, dragging myself through this parenting gig while they *(the 'gurus')* sit on their self-appointed thrones of wisdom, acting like they've unlocked the cheat codes to raising flawless mini-humans on three lettuce leaves and a chai-water to-go!

Of course, they would never allow *their* child to consume anything that wasn't organic, or let screen time exceed the *recommended daily allowance...* whatever that means.

Yes, it seems their glow, radiating with the kind of self-satisfaction usually reserved for *Geoff from HR (a fictional character who joined this book for no real reason but insists on turning up like my raging hormones)* - shines brighter than some fancy-dancy £200 pot of anti-ageing night cream.

Meanwhile, the rest of us are just over here, surviving on unintentionally cold coffee and calculating how much longer we can hide in the bathroom before someone panics and calls an ambulance, assuming we've passed out on the floor.

Wow, that quickly evolved into some parenting know-it-all guru-hating rant! Not sure where that came from. But then again, I'm not totally surprised. I am, after all, somewhat accustomed to delivering both internal and external rants.

Just the other day, some absolute pollock from the Water Board dumped his van in our community car park, in *the* most inconvenient, block-my-car-in-like-a-professional-turkey position available. I instinctively rallied the children to head out, and while doing so, had a full-blown "Have you absolutely no consideration for the people who actually live here??" shindig going on in my head.

But, of course, by the time I got outside, the aardvark had vanished, van and all, leaving me with nothing but a head full of unspent rage. So instead, I ranted to my poor daughter (I say poor, but she just laughs at me) about how inconsiderate he was... for moving *before* I could get out there and complain about how inconsiderate he was.

I'm sure at least one person can understand my pain here.
Or at least humour me over it!

Let's be real - as frequently demonstrated throughout this book, staying present is no easy task. I'm in my early *(clinging on to that part)* 40s, and I still get lost in my own brain on a daily basis. But I know I'm not the only one!

Did I mention unicorns are the national 'animal' of Scotland? Yes, really. I mean, I love Scotland (proud English settler of nearly ten years over here), but of all the majestic creatures to claim as a national symbol, y'all went with the mythical one?

Not a Highland cow? Not a stag? Nope. Just straight-up galloping into fantasy land!

Also, while we're here, can someone explain haggis? No? Fine. Leave me hanging, why don't you!

And just like that, we're back in the room!

I'd love to say that little detour was purely for dramatic effect…*(insert extra dramatic pause)*... and, well, maybe it was. Kind of. But more than that, it was a *reenactment* of my uncontrollable mind wandering. My distractedness in its finest. My free association with absolutely nothing relevant… And so on.

As I've probably hinted at *(or flat-out announced, repeatedly)*, I'm about 98% certain I have ADHD. Not the diagnosed kind, of course, because adult assessments via our local NHS are now about as accessible as Narnia. Unless you already tick a very specific set of boxes, the system politely slams the door and suggests you just... get on with it.

Private assessments exist, sure. But unless I fancy remortgaging the house or selling a kidney, that door is firmly shut too.

So here I am, winging it through daily life with a cocktail of suspected neurodivergence, a heroic caffeine habit, and sleep deprivation that predates TikTok. It's no wonder my brain behaves like an exhausted toddler with a megaphone and no impulse control.

You too? Bring it home, Mamas and Papas of the winging it club!

You all rock, with or without the extra fun genetics! You are my champions. My unmasked (because this was written post-COVID) heroes, and you deserve some deep recognition!

But even without those little bonus features, staying actively present is tough.

It's not a skill we're magically born with or something that downloads into our system on our second birthday *(although, let's be honest, that microchip would be useful).* Instead, it's a journey. A slow, sometimes frustrating, fork-in-the-road journey that requires patience, understanding, and a whole lot of persistence.

For children on the Autism or ADHD spectrum, as well as their families, it can be an especially long road, filled with small victories, setbacks, and constant learning.

Yes, *I know*, that sounds like something straight out of a parenting handbook! A cliche of parenting pats on the back, followed up with a gold star for doing your best. But I am one of *those* parents who struggled with this issue for years.

Believe me when I say, I've begged and cried to my son, shouting in utter despair, *"Why won't you just listen to me?"* Heck, I'm almost certain that at some point, my neighbours have sat bolt upright with a bewildered *"Why aren't I listening?"* expression, as my voice bellowed through the walls!

And it worked… hardly ever. That's the solid truth of it. In fact, I'd say it ranked pretty high on my list of parenting fails, right next to, "*My child stood in something funky, however, I'm just gonna play dumb in this rather nice cafe*", and "*Why are you eating the cat food? Hang on, is that cat food? Actually… Never mind. I don't want to know!*"

What I have learned, however, is that,

> *There is no point in punishing a child for struggling with skills they haven't yet figured out.*

And that is probably the biggest, most valuable parent-to-parent advice you will ever hear.

Let's be real - expecting your child to correct a problem they don't know exists is like pinpointing the reason your newborn bundle of DNA is screaming at 3am… Again. You've got around four and a half seconds before the wailing escalates into an opera performance that will likely wake the neighbours and their dog. And he will, because he's a 2ft furry jerk, unleash a howling symphony that ignites a blaze of angry zombies.

Remember those days? Yeah, me too, like a punch to the face! It wasn't fun, or *'cute'* like in the movies.

But then life isn't. Instead, it's messy and confusing, overwhelming and excessively demanding, especially for our kids. And once I realised this, once I stopped fighting against my son's way of seeing the world, and started working *with* it, things got a lot easier for everyone.

That doesn't mean the hard stuff disappeared. But it did mean fewer battles, fewer tears, and, most importantly, fewer instances of me wanting to yeet *(one of my son's favourite funny words!)* myself into the nearest bush.

Yes, I wholeheartedly advocate for taking the easier path. We should hop, skip, and run down it if need be *(because running uphill is a lot of effort)*. We should do a crazy chicken dance, pull out all the crazies. And shout '*Shiver me timbers'* like a pirate that's escaped a cruise ship cabaret. A chicken pirate. A chi-rate? A pir-ken?

I should add that I'm completely high on legal drugs right now. The medicine cabinet has been raided and my sense of 'up' is currently wobbling like an overset jelly…

Can you overset jelly? I don't know. But it sounds good.

The family has been hit by what I can only describe as the plague of 2025. It may only be March, but I am schizophrenically sure this has been sent over from some Sweet 'n' Sour Chicken lab, likely concealed in several dozen pairs of 'Sevi' jeans, with the sole purpose of wiping out a large chunk of humanity.

"Go to the doctors", you're probably thinking, or chanting through means of telepathy. Thanks. You're the best!

But I, a sleep-deprived Mama of two, would almost certainly be subjected to experimental testing if I sought medical advice, due to my unnatural levels of resilience, caked in high concentrations of caffeine, that somehow mean I am still standing. Well, sitting. But at least partially still 'with it.'

Behold, for I am at one with the mentally exhausted pigeon brigade. I am in awe of the orange-flavoured cat who sleeps not three feet away from me.

And I am determined to write today (despite barely managing one chapter in the past week), even if my effort, along with last week's, ends up being nothing more than fever-fueled drivel that future-me will have to rewrite... If and when my brain stops feeling like a deflated blow-up doll left abandoned in a skip behind a questionable nightclub.

And on that disturbing thought...

Have you ever zoned out *(the irony after my last rambling interlude!)* so hard mid-conversation that you suddenly realise you've nodded in agreement to something potentially catastrophic? Like, you're half-listening, making all the right noises, and then, bam! You've somehow agreed to host this year's community bake sale, foster a goat, or take part in some '*fun run*' that absolutely won't be fun at all.

Yeah. Me as well, far too many times.

But if someone were to ask why you weren't listening, you could probably cobble together a reasonable excuse.

- *Oh, sorry, I was just watching something on TV.*
- *I was thinking about that meeting tomorrow.*
- *I was internally debating whether penguins have knees, and honestly, that took priority.*

Sure, you might get an exasperated sigh, or a *"Why do I even bother?"* eye roll, but at least you're socially equipped to bluff your way out of it. No one's going to revoke your access to the snack cupboard for lack of effort.

But for our neurodivergent kids? That's a bucket-load of *'Good luck getting even a half-baked reason out of them'* served on ice.

Truth is, our small fries don't usually register the *'when'* and *'why'* of checking out. It's an autopilot response, like breathing, or instantly gagging at a new food before it's even hit their tongue. And the odds of you or me figuring out why they've disengaged from the world? About as promising as me walking past a *'Wet Paint'* sign without poking it *(come on, we've all done that at some point!)*

So what's the solution? How do we turn our zoning out zombies into cherubs of conversation, consideration and... (*I've run out of C words. Erm, Charm? Charisma? Capability? I don't know, but you get the point.)*

Well, according to some people *(you know, the all-knowing, ever-wise, probably childless parenting 'expert' kind of people I pitched a tantrum over earlier),* the answer is simple - just prioritise the conversation over everything else.

Oh! Of course! Silly me. I'll just hit the magical *'prioritize'* button in my child's brain, right next to the one that makes them remember not to run up the hallway, and directly above the setting that prevents them from licking condensation off the window.

Brilliant. Problem solved. Except, oh wait - real life doesn't work like that. If it did, I wouldn't have spent twenty-seven minutes trying to convince my son that, yes, the pasta does taste the same whether it's in dinosaur shape or boring adult tube form.

And yet, I had to do exactly that last week. Because logic? Yeah, it's selective. What makes perfect sense to us often doesn't land the same way in their world. Or if it does, it probably won't by the beginning of next week!

But do you know what *does* work? Subliminal messaging. Brain training from an alternate dimension. Hypnosis of the chicken. You know the one…

"When I click my fingers, you shall wake up, flap around the room clucking, and peck at 'seeds'. Your name is Dorothy. You have no memory of your past life. Only an unshakable urge to scratch at the carpet. Also, Christmas dinner is in eleven days, and, not to get your wings in a twist but, you are the guest of honor…"

OK, I'm not exactly a master of mind tricks. If I were, I'd have already programmed my emotionally charged ostrich to flip an inside-out t-shirt the right way round, accept that bananas in their solid form are *not* a conspiracy. And, just maybe, actually listen when I say, *'Keep your head up and the water won't go in your eyes'* every… single… time… I wash his hair.

But instead of being gifted with divine parental powers, I've been handed sarcasm, hair ties, and the ability to overshare with complete strangers.

So let me paint you a picture instead. Not with brushes, obviously - I don't have time for hobbies. But with words.

Think of it like a Willy Wonka adventure… only with less chocolate and significantly fewer unpaid orange immigrants crammed into questionable working conditions.

Ready? Let's go.

✦✦✦ - ✦✦✦

You've stumbled into the world's worst party.
We're talking a cringe-worthy, zero stars on TrustPilot, "Did I wrong a witch in a past life?" kind of party.

The bass is hammering through your chest, each beat rattling your ribs like a trapped budgie trying to escape. And the air is thick, humid with body heat, stale beer, and the unmistakable tang of sweat-drenched polyester.

Flashing neon slices through the dark, burning patterns into your retinas. And that relentless strobe makes everything feel surreal and disjointed.

Someone is right in your ear, shouting in a terrible fake French accent, because they've mistaken your beanie for a beret. Their breath is hot and smells of cheap vodka and regret. And you want to turn away, but there's nowhere to go.

Your skin is prickling, hot, clammy, and stretched too tight. You can feel the sweat gathering at the base of your neck, rolling down your spine in slow, itchy trails. You just need to leave. To breathe. But the crowd is shifting, pressing in, as the sea of strangers moves in waves that have no rhythm, no pattern.

The exit was there a second ago, wasn't it? Now it's gone, swallowed by the bodies, the noise, the chaos. Your heart is hammering. Your breathing is shallow. And the walls feel like they're closing in…

✦✦✦ - ✦✦✦

Now I'm no expert, but I get the distinct impression that, for a lot of neurodivergent kids and even adults, *this* is on par with how life's expectations can feel. It's too loud. Too chaotic. Too much. And trying to hold a conversation in the middle of that sensory onslaught? Yeah, it's not that they *won't* listen - it's that they *can't*.

So, what was my solution? I can sense your burning anticipation (*as opposed to any burning precipitation from down below… which would obviously need medical advice rather than my idiocies!)*

I know you're probably expecting some grand resolution here. Some life-changing fix I've been keeping up my sleeve. And I get it - I did kind of open this chapter suggesting that it might, in some far-fetched way, be helpful.

But I'm no magician. There is no white rabbit about to emerge, fluffy tail first. And my offerings are about as impressive as a glitter bomb at a funeral - chaotic, messy, and guaranteed to ruin someone's day!

See, I can't even be serious about funerals! It's not that my mouth engages before my brain. Oh no, my brain is fully strapped in for this ride. It's complicit, like an eighteen-year-old stripper, just trying to make enough money to get through Uni.

I just cope better with difficult situations through humour. Inappropriate, *get me banned from Sunday school* humour. Actually, no - that's a lie. I never went to Sunday school. And this twisted sense of amusement? It only came to light when I had kids.

It's like, while birthing an 8.6lb wonderbeast (not to be confused with the orange wildebeest), I finally found my voice. An outlet for all the trauma, all the misery dumped on my young, unsuspecting soul. And instead of gracefully unpacking it in therapy like a normal person, I reached a '*pluck it twice and shake for gold*' state of mind.

I am, however, going to lead you down the path with false promises of candy… *no, scrub that…* With the emotional clickbait of nine hours, uninterrupted sleep! *(Seriously, slap that on the side of a white van and I'm climbing in with zero hesitation and a travel mug of coffee I might actually get to drink warm for a change.)*

Why? Because I'm kind of into this two-part, helping-you-helping-me cha-cha slide. And let's be honest - long chapters are not my thing.

So I'll see you in the next bit, where we actually try to *solve* some of this nonsense.

Maybe.

Chapter 10: Are You Even Listening

A not-so-expert guide to actually hearing each other.

I didn't start off looking for a strategy. I was just trying to understand why my son couldn't, or seemingly wouldn't, just listen to me like I asked.

Not in a *"He's being difficult on purpose"* kind of way - I knew it wasn't that. But still, I found it more confusing than the Dachshund X Spaniel I met the other day... Like how?

How could he recall an obscure fact about the latest food blenders from a random YouTube video he watched three weeks ago, complete with hand gestures and unnecessary sound effects, yet completely *'ignore'* me asking him to put his socks on... ten seconds ago?

I mean, the brain is clearly working. It's *active.* It has storage. It just doesn't seem to store anything *I* say unless it involves biscuits, Roman emperors, or the phrase *"limited screen time."* It's like I'm speaking from inside a tunnel made of static and penne-pasta-repellent, shouting into the void while he's out here quoting historical facts with perfect comedic timing.

So, I did what any mentally maxed-out, biscuit-bribing parent with a WiFi connection would do - I researched. A lot.

I trawled through parenting forums, got lost in a black hole of expert blogs, and skimmed more academic PDFs than I care to admit. And somewhere in the chaos, I stumbled into the science-y stuff - the kind with complicated diagrams and words like *'executive dysfunction'* and *'cognitive regulation'* that made my brain feel like a deep-fried banana.

As you know, I live in Scotland. I'm not Scottish, but rather just a humble resident of this little corner of haggis-roaming land.

And while it's not quite a full-blown dietary revolution, the folk on this side of the border do seem willing to deep fry just about anything. I'm talking burgers, pizzas, pickled eggs, and of course, the mighty Mars bar, just to name a few!

Ye'r a' a bunch o' nutters! In th' best wey, o' coorse!

(Not that I'm stereotyping my Scottish friends, family or associates !)

But underneath all the jargon, something clicked. It turns out, the brain has this *'decision-making mode.'* A moment where it stops just passively existing and actually *engages*.

And while I'm not about to give a TED Talk on neural pathways *(mainly because I'll either mistype or completely misinterpret something. And in some cruel twist of the universe, it'll end up in the lap of a Neurological Expert who'll gleefully call me out in the Mail on Sunday. No thanks!)*, this idea stuck with me.

So, I turned it into something simple.
Playful. And surprisingly effective.

(Drum roll please….!)

Listening Ears or Lazy Ears? That's the phrase I came up with.

Yes, it sounds silly, and it kind of is, but it works. It nudges his brain out of autopilot and into that elusive '*decision-making mode*'. And by doing so, instead of drifting in the zone-out zone, his thoughts are gently steered toward picking a lane.

Not in a stern, *"Answer me now!"* kind of way, but more like offering two clear paths and letting him choose which one to walk. Far better than mentally joyriding the North Coast 500 *(which, incidentally, is an excellent way to waste a couple of days, complete with winding roads, cliffs, lochs, wild sheep with no fear of death, and more bends than my moral compass at 8am on a Sunday morning!)*

Instead of my usual dramatic *"Are you even listening to me?!"*, which, let's be honest, was just me venting into the void, I started asking, *"Listening Ears or Lazy Ears?"*

Note, I don't ask it from halfway across the room while he's mid-YouTube deep diving. Instead, I wait. I connect. Gain eye contact, use a gentle tone, maybe even a goofy raised eyebrow, or a jump on the spot to grab attention.

And yes, sometimes I have to repeat myself, three or four times, if he's deep diving the Mariana Trench of obscure facts and doesn't have the mental Wi-Fi to resurface yet. But when he's ready, he'll look up and repeat *"Listening Ears"*, while signing the word *'listening'* with Makaton. (Quick YouTube search will show you how if you fancy adding that in.)

And that moment?
That's him choosing to be present.
That's his *"Yes, I'm here".*
And giving me his full attention.

Don't get me wrong - sometimes he picks '*Lazy Ears',* which might sound cheeky. But honestly, it's a high-five, you're doing an awesome job, proud mama moment.

Why? Because he's not ignoring me, or trying to be rude. He's self-regulating.

(Cue the silent head-tilt from the smug parenting elite - the ones who'd sooner die than let a child think for themselves, and who are already muttering something about "boundaries" while passive-aggressively wiping oat milk foam from their ethically sourced travel cups!)

But here's the thing - if I force it, I might as well go have a cuppa with Monty the houseplant. *He's* more of the strong, silent type, and not prone to fact-spamming me with kitchen gadget rundowns!

Give my son a minute, though? Let the hyperfocus wind down? He'll circle back and join the conversation, fully present. And for me, that's a win.

Now, will this magic little phrase work for every child? Who knows. Maybe not. But the bones of it, the *choice*, the *permission to wait*, the lack of *'nagging voice',* that's where the power is.

And if *"Listening Ears or Lazy Ears"* feels too cutesy for your teen, and likely to earn you an earth-quaking eye-roll, slammed door, or *'lame parent of the year'* social media share, no stress.

Tweak it.
Make your own version.
Use a hand signal.
A weird dance move.
A spontaneous rap debut...

Yo, listen up, kiddo, gather 'round
Your Mum's talkin', put that phone down, no more scrollin' around
You're missin' life, and it's passin' you by
Too busy likin', commentin', and gettin' them likes high

You got chores to do, and a future to claim
But you're stuck in a screen, and it's causin' you shame
Your priorities wrong, your focus is blurred
You need to look up, and let the world be heard!

(Ok, maybe not, unless you're a freestyling pro, which I am clearly not! No need to point it out – that's just rude! Honestly, I'm out here dropping questionable parenting bars, and you're gonna call me out? Pfft. Critics, man!)

Or... mime it out in sock puppets if you want - whatever helps your kid check back in *without* feeling like they're being summoned to a board meeting. Because this isn't about making them listen.

It's about helping them choose to engage in a way that works for their beautifully wired, sometimes chaotic, always worthy brains.

And if that doesn't work? Well... there's always interpretive dance.

Side note: *Monty has endured more heart-aching monologues than most therapy dogs. He's not great, but he's doing his best. And I'm now considering giving him a promotion to Emotional Support Foliage.*

Notes From the Edge

24th February 2025 ♡

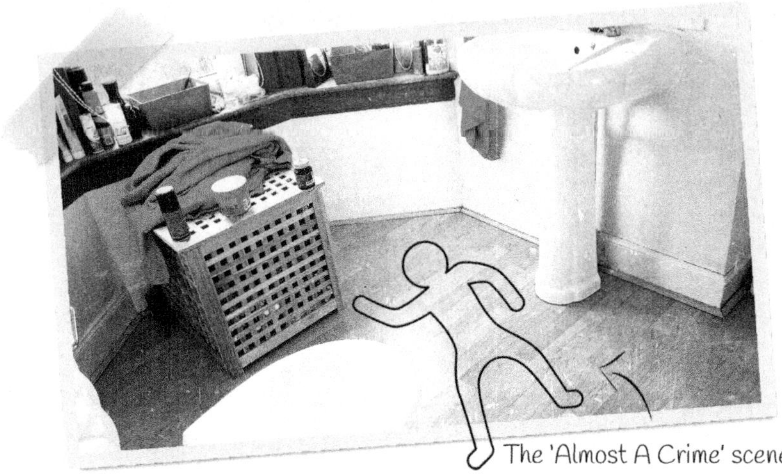

The 'Almost A Crime' scene!

Why do I always end up writing these diary entries on a Monday? Well, because Mondays are, without fail, a sheep show of a day. Not because of my kids, or even the soul-sucking amount of adulting required of me.

Oh no. Mondays and I are just locked in a psychological war zone.

Take today, for example. It was nine something AM, as in the morning, as in the worst part of Monday. And I found myself hopping around in the bathroom like a manatee out of water.

I was attempting to get my jeans on without sitting down, because, well, the floor was cold and undignified to get back up from. And so, the hopping-about jeans-on dance was the only other option. We've all done it. And those of you who say you haven't? Well, you're lying.

On what was probably the third 'fearing for my life as the sink is nearby and concussion from unplanned head-first contact is a real possibility' endeavour, I looked down into my jeans. And to my absolute horror, saw a large gaping hole peering up at me

Not the way I wanted to start my Monday. They are my go-to jeans, my live-and-die denims.

Only, I've leaned on them a little too hard, maxed out their fibre loyalty, and now, they've betrayed me in the worst way possible. There is a hole where no woman wants a hole. A draft where draft excluders should exist. An unwanted peep show from down below.

Only... The hole I spied? Yeah. *It was the leg hole.* You know, the hole that's *meant* to be there, specifically designed for my foot to slide through. Turns out, I just hadn't consumed enough coffee to realise that yet.

And that kind of set the tone for my day.

Mr D, the magical, now somewhat mystical Mr D, is off. Again. He's kindly rearranged our piano class for Wednesday. Lovely, right? Except now Wednesday will feel like a Monday. And the chance of me meeting the rest of Wednesday's criteria without having at least seventeen mini breakdowns is fading fast.

I'll be relying almost entirely on my almost-teen daughter to railroad me into an early dinner and late-night drama class drive. But given that she's just wandered in to grab a wet paper towel to scrub *Sharpie ink* off an art project?

Yeah. Let's just say, the odds are *not* in our favour.

We have, however, tried to resurrect Music Monday ♬★.° with an at-home piano lesson, which was reasonably 'didn't-lose-our-sheep' successful. But if anyone is delusional enough to think that means I can teach my son the *Beethoven way of life* from the comfort of my sofa... yeah, you're very much mistaken.

I am *not* musically inclined. I have to Google every tiny conundrum and pray that YouTube will come through like some divine symphony saviour.

Mr. D's job? Yeah, that's very, very secure ▶ •ıı|ıı|ıı|ıı|

My sanity, however, is less so. Right now, I'm perched in the *posh officium*... (That's Latin for 'fancy office'. Why Latin? No real reason, other than I'm rambling. And it's not even posh. It's an open hallway with a desk and a *Kallax unit* from IKEA. Real classy!)

My coffee dregs have gone cold, the orange-flavoured cat is making strange Mogwai noises in his sleep. And my son is stimming away whilst playing on his tablet downstairs. Honestly, between them, they could drop an album.

No, scratch that... *record some 'soul-healing soundscape' downloads* (because records and CDs aren't a thing anymore!) It would likely appeal to some new age enthusiasts who'd say it spoke to their inner deepness, or their little left toe, or some other nonsense.

And me? I'm just *sitting in the middle of it all*, the cold coffee, the background noise, the chaos, and feeling a little lost.

Maybe it's just one of *those* days. Or maybe it's the aftermath of the weekend catching up with me. We had two back-to-back additional needs stay-and-play sessions, which, if you've never experienced one, are basically like being in a hostage situation.

There's lots of screaming. Multiple torture devices in the form of loud and offensive toys. And food you're scared to eat in case it's been poisoned, aka sneezed on by a passing child.

You spend the majority of the event clock-watching and trying not to make eye contact with other hostages, as you have no real way of knowing which side they're on. And when the doors finally open, amidst the fresh, cold, wet Scottish weather, a break for freedom is made by one and all!

My son had a blast, for the most part. But he's now emotionally burnt out. And I get that. Peopling is hard. We, as a family, are not naturally social, what with my daughter's anxiety and my son's often misunderstood needs. I find it hard to force them out into the world, where they often stumble from the overwhelming big feelings. And to be honest, we'd all rather curl up on the sofa with hot chocolates and a good movie ⊹ ☕

But I know that's not preparing them for life. And so, we push on, even when it's super uncomfortable.

That's something I tell both my kids a lot – get comfortable with being uncomfortable. Because guess what? Life doesn't come with a fast-forward button, a skip intro, or a magical 'opt out of awkward situations' clause. Instead, it throws you a tantrum in Tesco, a weird smell in the car, or a maths worksheet designed by actual demons. And you still have to show up, no matter how itchy, squirmy, or rage-scream-y it is.

I tell them: you don't have to *love* it. You just have to *live* through it.

And if you can do that, not run, not melt, not yell into the void (OK, maybe a little), then you've already won something far better than a gold star. You've built the muscle for real life. And real life, as we know, is basically one long awkward moment in different outfits.

Ah, that almost sounded poetic! I might print it off and laminate it and then... do nothing with it, other than file it under my cup of coffee. Good intentions and all that jazz, speaking of which, here are three good things that did happen today...

1. We made the most of the brief burst of sunshine and took my son scootering. It rained while we were out, but I don't think he noticed
2. There was just enough cherry jam left for my round of toast at lunch
3. My son finished his handwriting workbook, which we started over 6 months ago – pencil work isn't his 'thing', and so we just plugged away at it, little by little, and got there in the end, -ˏˋ ★ ˎˊ-

> "Believe in yourself and all that you are. Know that there is something inside you that is greater than any obstacle."
> – Christian D. Larson

Chapter 11: Explain Yourself

Instructions not included
(but strongly advised!)

No one told me that having kids, and more specifically, having a kid with extra extras, would lead me to a Mexican standoff, complete with cheesy Doritos and a spicy attitude, over how to stack dominoes.

Yes, you did read that right.

For probably five years now, my emotionally charged ostrich has been a full-blown domino enthusiast. What started as innocent stacking quickly spiraled him into a pyramid-building junkie. And before I knew it, we were smuggling American domino hoards through airport security, tucked into my husband's suitcases like contraband.

Customs would have had a field day when asking, *"Sir, do you have anything to declare?"* And in my head, he'd mutter in reply,

"Yes. Kind of. But it's not what you think… Unless it's your thing too? You see, there's this kid. He's not mine, but he sort of is - a whole step kid situation, no DNA involved, but plenty of itchy socks and emotional trauma…
Anyway, he sent me money to bring home dominoes. Not the pizza, though that would've been easier to explain…
No, these are premium, limited-edition, American dominoes. The kind that makes British dominoes cry. I'm talking smooth side, crisp fall, and colours so vibrant they basically yell 'freedom!' when they topple…
And before you ask, no. I'm not OK. I've been on three flights, my pants are cutting off circulation to my will to live, and I'm carrying the hopes and dreams of a small autistic child who'll emotionally combust if this plastic cargo doesn't make it home!"

Ah, the joy! But our lifestyle choices do not stop there, for this almost cult-like fixation. Oh no. When buying new sofas last year, a footstool with lift-up storage space was added to the bundle to house this obsession!

Yes, a well-known brand, let's call them *Sofas and Jokers*, clocked us the second we walked in. Parent with tired eyes, nervous credit card, and a child who, of course, had to question, "*But where will my dominoes live?"* as he bounced up and down on six different mock-up living rooms.

They, the laughing hyenas, upsold us like we were gullible lottery winners. And in doing so, probably secured their annual bonus scheme holiday in the process. Yes, I could practically hear the clink of piña coladas as they rang up our order and waved us off with a "*Best of luck with your… domino bunker?"*

And, twelve months later, we still have a stylish grey suite, a faint smell of existential regret, and a footstool that holds the remains of my parental dignity, as well as a lifetime supply of dominoes… *Again, not the pizza.*

But that's not the point here. No, the real issue is that I, in my infinite wisdom *(aka the chaotic parenting energyist)*, failed to assess the *millions* of theoretical outcomes that could explode from launching into a domino challenge with my rule-led, domino-obsessed child, whom I birthed nearly nine years ago.

Or, to put it simply *(yes, I do like a carry-on with ridiculously long-winded rambles, but I know that sometimes, a 'cut to the chase' insert is easier on the brain)*, I didn't fully explain the rules of our game, the restrictions and expectations for each build, or how to determine the winner.

And that pretty much sums up at least half of my waking day.

This child of mine is chaos wrapped in cuddles - a whirlwind of energy with a fragile GPS signal. At first glance, he's like a walking talking IKEA desk, with three extra screws, and absolutely no sign of the *how-to-build-him* doofer. You know, the *thingy-ma-jig*. The official parenting *what's-it-called*. That *mythical scroll of guidance*, which he seemed to lose on his way out of the womb, just to spice things up.

But that's the thing - he does need instructions. They're the safety harness holding us in as the day whips past at unsafe speeds. Without them, the system crashes, the screen goes blue, and we're all just passengers on a derailed roller coaster designed by someone who spilt coffee on the blueprint and skipped the safety briefing entirely.

Give him a clear set of steps, and he thrives. Miss one crucial point, and suddenly we're in a courtroom-style debate over why I didn't specify that the domino build *must* begin at the westernmost corner of the footstool.

And right on cue, we interrupt this program to complain about the 'totally illogical' format of this six times table quiz.

Whilst his workbook on the whole is acceptable, with bright colours, a good backstory, and no fancy fonts (bonus!), it has *zero* autism-tolerance baked in. Not even a sprinkle. And that, my friends, is a recurring issue we've slammed into throughout our home-ed journey.

Is it my fault for not insisting he *'gets to grips'* with this jumbled chaos of a learning style? That he just buckle down and stop his nonsense?

No. Absolutely not. His brain is logical. Patterned. Rhythmic.

But that also means, when he's faced with the six times table, in a hacked-up ham sandwich kind of order, it's like asking Mozart to compose symphonies with a xylophone missing three keys, and a kazoo shoved up his left nostril.

This sort of scattergun nonsense sets him up to fail. It's like a paperback equivalent of saying *"Go bake a Victoria sponge!"* but hiding the eggs and flour, throwing the butter out the window, and yelling *"Surprise assessment!"* halfway through weighing the sugar!

And yes, in an ideal world, I'd love to write a full curriculum, where each page follows a pattern, one logical step at a time, with real-world references, and absolutely no maniac-inspired questions. But unfortunately, I am neither qualified nor emotionally stable enough to dedicate the next ten to fifteen years of my life to authoring that series.

It would be lovely if someone did? Hint hint!

Although my emotionally charged ostrich has his quirks, like getting up at exactly 7:56am, or pleading with humanity whenever he sees a queue, I've come to realise that in the grand scheme of things, our challenges are somewhat manageable, especially when I think about what some families quietly endure.

And I know there will be parents who read this book and wonder what on earth I'm moaning about. That I've got it easy. That I clearly don't understand what real, deep-end-of-the-spectrum struggles look like.

That I'm making a Broadway musical out of a speck of mildly inconvenient glitter. A hostage situation out of... *well, actually, no.* There were no real hostages, unless you count my son's tablet, which was briefly held under Mum Law when he was acting like a lazy primate with Wi-Fi entitlement issues.

But honestly? If you are one of those parents, you are justified in your thinking. I don't know your life. I haven't walked your paths or fought your battles for support, for services, for the tiniest crumb of recognition in a system that seems to run on denial and budget cuts.

But just to be clear, if I were trying to compete, it wouldn't be in the suffering Olympics. No, thank you. I'd rather enter a strawberry cheesecake showdown, or a race to see who can achieve the most structurally unstable messy bun in seven seconds flat... Because if life must be a competition, let it be one with frosting and a hair tie hanging on for dear life!

It's true - our journeys likely contrast in so many ways. Yours is maybe steeper, rockier, with potholes big enough to swallow your last shred of patience. Or maybe it's softer in places, decorated with gentle hills, and only the occasional landslide.

Maybe you have a village *(yes, I said it, the on-trend term of the decade)*, complete with a tag-team of babysitters, therapy recommendations on speed dial, and friends who bring wine and biscuits without being asked.

Or maybe, like us, you're winging it mostly alone, Googling symptoms at 2am and wondering whether you're doing any of it right. And sometimes, the scariest part of that? It's realising that no one's coming to tell you if you are.

> *Our paths, while different in terrain, are still moving through the same storm.*

We are all walking *(or limping, or dragging ourselves face-down over Lego)* through this together. So before you toss this book onto one of those fancy fire pits in a blaze of mildly unhinged fury, see it for what it is - my peace offering.

A goodwill gesture in a world that so often lacks grace, patience, and the ability to just be decent. A paper hug from one chaotic, over-caffeinated, under-qualified parent to another.

No, we may not share the exact same chaos, but we speak the same language… which is more than can be said for my *'summer body goals'* and the daily Nutella-on-toast cravings!

Being disgracefully honest, the idea of a two-piece swimsuit is now less *'smoking hot'* and more *'dumpster fire in flip-flops'.* Because at almost forty-two, I've found myself in an intense game of tug-'o'-war with middle age. And for the most part, I'm being dragged across the line of self-respect, saggy backside first.

You're shocked by this, I can tell. In your mind, I'm a vision of serene motherhood with matching socks and an exfoliated soul. But no. What you actually get is a midlife crisis, held together with dry shampoo, caffeine, and high-waisted hold-it-all-in jeans from ASDA.

I'm like an angel sent from heaven, only it was Hampshire, back in '83.

And instead of wings, I come equipped with body art, greying hair, and a short fuse for imbeciles who think smugness is a parenting technique.

Which brings me neatly to the next guest: let's give a warm, passive-aggressive round of applause as we welcome Sharon to the table *(because I'm done blaming everything on the Karens).*

She's from our local incontinence team and, last summer, treated me to a twenty-three-minute phone call that felt less like support and more like a polite scolding disguised as *'professional concern.'* Her tone was flat, her advice patronising, and her empathy somewhere between *'complete factory reset'* and *'customer service operator on a Friday at 4:59pm.'*

But her pièce de résistance? Her freshly whipped buttercream icing on the cake? Her two-penny worth that no one asked for?

"You're just not trying hard enough. You're not making any real effort to toilet train your son. He'll get it when you actually commit to the program."

Oh, Sharon. Sweetheart. I've committed harder than an 80s porn star growing out his signature moustache. I've read the books. I've tried the charts. I've mopped up puddles that only got noticed when tiny wet footprints started creating modern art across the kitchen tiles. I've begged, bribed, sobbed in toilet cubicles, and nearly ruptured something doing celebratory dances over half a teaspoon of wee in the right place.

Believe me, if there were a shortcut that let me pass Go and collect two hundred Monopodollars instead of changing between three and eight pull-ups a day, I'd have laminated that sucker and tattooed it on my forearm, in some *"Stick that up your jacksie!"* celebration.

And yet, instead, I'm having to explain myself, yet again.

To justify. To defend the mess, the exhaustion, the endless loop of effort. All to another clipboard-wielding monkey working through a tick-box exercise like a bonus points scheme.

There's no genuine curiosity.
No pause to consider the human behind the paperwork.
It's just another day.
Another file.
Another parent to tell how they're doing it all wrong

Urgh! That felt good to get out of my system! There's only so many times I can rant at the cat, the empty bubble bath bottles, or my own echo in the car whilst trying to rewire the footwell lights that I stupidly dislodged... again!

Venting is good for the soul! Not my neighbours, but the soul!

If it's not a nosy Neddy dishing out unsolicited *"back in my day"* comments, it's a bus-stop battleaxe serving side-eye like it's an Olympic event. If it's not the tactless specialist who thinks their degree trumps lived experience, it's the cluster of emotionally constipated fruit-wielders in Tesco, clutching their bananas like they've just witnessed a crime.

Then there's the friends and family with their *'helpful'* suggestions we never asked for. The media reminding us we're not doing enough. And just when we think we've survived the outside noise, in comes the quiet heartache and relentless self-doubt, clawing away at whatever belief we've got left.

At times, I wish it were legal to carry a paintball gun. Just one. Just to aim and fire at the puppets of contempt, those who act like they invented parenting, and we're nothing more than poorly mimicking their greatness.

I'm not talking about a full-on attack. No. Merely a bright red splatter, right across their pristine John Lewis jumper, just to offer a tiny, unwashable glimpse of what it's like to be marked, targeted, and reduced to a moment of judgment in someone else's oh-so-important day.

Oh, that got deep fast, didn't it? One minute I'm talking about pornstars. And the next, shooting random people so red floods their clothes. My bad!

To clarify: I've never held a paintball gun. The idea of shooting someone isn't a burning fantasy. And nor is the thought of prison food, as I've now mentioned once or twice.

I just want a little more empathy in the world. A little less sanctimonious bull-sheep. And a fighting chance for our kids to be accepted, welcomed, and celebrated, without us having to justify their existence to every Sharon with a laminated flowchart and a superiority complex.

Today, my boy and I were talking about friendships, about how he so freely walks up to other kids and asks, *"Do you want to be friends?"* And how, for the next thirty to sixty minutes, they reign as best buddies, playing like they've known each other their whole lives.

It's genuinely endearing, the innocence. But I did gently suggest that maybe, just maybe, he could try asking, *"Do you want to play together?"* instead, and assess whether that person would be a good friend fit. After all, no one wants to make a soft-play promise only to discover their new *'best friend'* is wearing odd socks on purpose, or throws elbows at toddlers in moments of rage!

Truth be told, I rarely find a good fit in other people. I'm outspoken. I bite back when pushed. And at times, come across as rude, even when that's the furthest thing from my intention.

I'm just not built for sugar-coating *(as noted in Chapter 2)* or awkward small talk. I don't do well with surface-level smiles or people who flinch at honesty. I'm intense, and messy, and sometimes too much.

And that's why, for me, new friendships are hard.

I told my son, it's like a fire, burning deep down. For the most it keeps my soul warm, but sometimes, without warning, that fire gets out of control *(no, not in a beat people with poles way - I'm not that unstable!)* Some people just seem to fuel my fire, to poke sticks around the edge, and then wonder why they get burnt.

And my kid? He said he *gets* that feeling. And that meant more than I can put into words. Because for him, understanding emotions, especially the kind you can't see or touch, doesn't always come easily. His world makes sense through visuals, through things he can watch, build, or see in motion.

But in this moment?
There was none of that.
It was just the two of us, chatting away as I drove into town.
And somehow, he still understood.

He told me he feels that fire too - not in the exact words I'd used, but in his own way. Jumbled, a little tangled, but clear enough that I knew exactly what he meant. He feels it when everything's too loud, too fast, too confusing. When nothing makes sense and his brain can't keep up. The surge of emotions builds so quickly, he can't hold them back - they just erupt.

And I see it. I see it in the way his legs swing, his feet lash out, his hands grab at his hair or ears. And the shrieks of *"I don't understand"* over and over again.

We talked about the flood that often follows, or sometimes, crashes in on its own. The tears that roll down his cheeks. The breath that won't slow down. The way his whole world suddenly feels like a half-finished drawing, scribbled over in and torn up in frustration before he ever got to finish it.

I get it, kid. I really do. I get those big feelings, the kind that fill up your chest and leave no room for anything else. And I get how hard they are to work through.

But we will. I promise.

You bring out the best in me… Ok, maybe not my absolute best at 8:04am when you shout, *"Mum! I need help!"* I mean, I've not even made eye contact with the orange-flavoured assassin at that point. From the depths of his sinister soul, he's already plotting chaos, usually while perched on something expensive, breakable, or forbidden.

But most of the time? You do. And that's enough to keep me going, even on those cloudy days.

We're not perfect. We're not polished. But we're doing this together, flaws, fire, floods, and all. And maybe that's where the real strength lies. Not in having it all figured out, but in holding onto each other while we try…

Cliche I know, but also, very real.

That's all I'll ever ask of you, kiddo, to try. Try to find a reason to smile, even on the heavy days. Try to hold onto a dream, no matter how far away it seems. And try to believe that no matter what, I'll always be here for you.

(Even if I'm hiding in the bathroom for five minutes of peace…!)

P.S. *Just in case you were wondering, I told the incontinence team worker to shove her "not trying hard enough" bull-sheep up her pompous derriere, preferably while dry-chewing her precious tick sheets.*

P.P.S. *Thanks to Pampers Ninjamas and Amazon Prime (not sponsored by the way), my ignored pleas for incontinence support were swiftly replaced by a glorious stack of pull-ups that actually fit. They arrived in under 24 hours and restored my son's confidence in one big-boy pants swoop. The revolution was Amazon-delivered*

Chapter 12: Socially Slothed Out

Because people-ing
can do one.

I really want to snuzzle up with a sloth. They're slow, sleepy little legends who speak to my soul in ways most humans never could. Just drifting through life at a leisurely crawl, looking slumbrous, and somehow making the *bare minimum effort*, look like a lifestyle choice.

So imagine my heartbreak when I found out that sloths, *my spiritual siblings in the art of doing less*, don't actually want to be snuggled like a Care Bear.

Nope. Turns out, they're not the chilled-out cuddle buddies I imagined. They're wild jungle introverts who find human contact *stressful*. Being held isn't relaxing for them; it's an anxiety-inducing horror show that can literally shorten their lifespan.

Which, in hindsight, only proves my point - I am, without a doubt, at one with the sloth. I mean, I don't exactly thrive on excessive human contact either, physical *or* mental.

Small talk? Nope.
Forced hugs (*with the exception of my kids*)? Please don't.
And let's be honest, there are days when just answering a WhatsApp, email, or phone call from that friend I meant to get back to last week feels like running a social marathon I never signed up for.

So, with that in mind, you can probably imagine the gut-wrenching misery that simmered in the pit of my stomach as I sat through two *excruciatingly* long hours at my son's recent ASN get-together, shin-a-ding-ding, thing.

Yes, we're talking the kind of misery that starts in your gut and slowly spreads to your soul, like emotional IBS, fuelled by lukewarm squash, forced cheerfulness, and the sinking realisation that you'd rather be anywhere else. Including a root canal. Or jury duty. Or the seventh circle of soft play.

That sounded way more dramatic than I'd intended, like an over-the-top intro of a horror movie, or the part in a West End play where someone 'dies' but takes a solid three minutes of exaggerated gasps and unnecessary limb flailing to do it.

I should be kinder about the whole initiative. And I will be, because it's a good thing, an *appreciated* thing by not just us but many, many families in the area. The program is run as a safe space, a once-a-month all-together designed for neurodiverse kids. A gathering of curious, beautiful minds, all eager to explore the world, but with the comfort of knowing they're surrounded by people who *get it*.

And my son? Well, he awkwardly enjoys it.

He dives headfirst into the chaos… until the chaos crashes right back into him.
He thrives on the collection of toys, the buzz, the excitement… until someone moves something out of place, and suddenly, that joy collapses into frustration.

And the noise? That endless hum of screams, laughter, and footsteps echoing off every surface? It sends his little heart racing, somewhere between pure euphoria and total distress.

I can see by the end of the two-hour stay-and-play session that he's burnt out. But then, so are most of the kids on the dance floor. The *one hundred and twenty minutes* of social interaction takes a toll. And that emotional rollercoaster they were already struggling to control? Yeah, it's about to take a sharp dive into the void.

But do you know what? Next month, I'll do it all over again.

I'll bundle my small human into the cocoon of not-yet-socially-accepted butterflies, and sit through another *one hundred and twenty minutes* of emotional carnage. And for that *one hundred and twenty minutes*, I'll do my utmost to glare and snarl at any human being above four feet tall that dares come near me!

I'm such a joy to be around… Not!

Actually, that's not quite true. There are a number of people whom I find myself in blissful peopleness with. Folk, I can *actually* be my weird and wonderful self around, who embrace my crazies without flinching and give me the space to just *be me.*

And those people? They're special. Not in a *lick-the-windows* kind of way - that's just weird. But more in a *big lump in my throat, "Wowzers, I'm lucky to have you - please don't ever leave me"* kind of way.

This shot was taken back in 2015, when my close friend, and talented photographer, John, and I were out in the bluebell fields for a modelling shoot.

He tragically passed away just a few months later from cancer. It still feels strange to say it. Sudden, unfair, heartbreaking – all of it. But in my head, and always in my heart, he'll be one of the good ones. My kind of human. The kind who didn't need to be loud to light up a room. The kind who could capture a moment and make you feel like magic lived in the everyday.

I'm just sad he never got to meet my son. I know they would have got on like a house on fire... no, I'll rephrase that... Like a pair of two-year-olds, eating blue Smarties on a sunny Friday afternoon. I would have tried to tell John off for leading my son down a mischievous path, but failed miserably. And instead, insisted that they give me all the orange ones!

If you've got those kinds of humans in your life, *hold on to them...* Not literally, though – *please* don't cling to their ankles while they're trying to get around the supermarket. That's how restraining orders happen.

But seriously, *make time for them* whenever you can.

There's a huge part of me that never wants to leave the house. Just let me live in pyjama bottoms and ten-year-old vest tops, watching the midget humans scurry beneath my second-floor window like panicked ants on a caffeine binge.

But I have kids. And kids need to be *peopled*. You know, shoved into society just enough that they either grow to love their community or vow to never partake in such ghastly nonsense as adults. *(I'm obviously hoping for the first. Preparing for the latter. And realistically? I'll happily accept somewhere in between!)*

But... What if my son doesn't find that same acceptance? What if, twenty years from now, he's faced with farmers at the door, armed with pitchforks and flaming torches at 4am?

Oh, wait! That was the film, Dracula. Never mind!

The point is *(yes, I do have one, surprisingly)* that social acceptance is something most of us crave. I don't care how roughty-toughty someone is pretending to be - we all want to feel the love! And no, I don't mean some trippy, 60s-inspired flower-power love fest. Or an awkward pat-down from a police officer after getting caught speeding under the moonlight.

I remember wrestling with that whole social acceptance dilemma when I was considering getting my chest tattooed. Yes, I was *that* person, back in 2021, who asked her awesome tattoo artist and friend to casually learn upon her bosom for approximately two and a half hours. And stab her like some dominatrix in latex gloves.

Yes, yes, that did happen. I had the bruises for weeks to prove it, and, you know, the tattoo, which was, and still is, flipping amazing! But it took a few months for me to pluck up the courage to get it done. Although I knew I wanted the inked-up cleavage, I was all too aware of the stigma that would be attached to it.

And more so, that my then-seven-year-old daughter would feel that burden. So we talked it through, she and I. And she told me to do it anyway. She told me, *"So what if they stare and judge, as long as you're happy then it doesn't matter"*. That was my kid, at seven years old.

Now, either she was born an *absolute legend (which she undoubtedly is, but that's not the point)*, or she'd already clocked what most adults haven't figured out yet, which was, no matter what you do, *haters gonna hate*.

And honestly? That was all the validation I needed to go live the life I deserved.

Now, I know in your head, I probably sit and throw out these chapters in a single day – cosied up in my office, children playing like cherubs, and not a soul (except for my furbabies in their nearby cat tree) disturbing my creative flow.

But the reality is very frogging different. And as such, this next part was written the next day from the bit you just read. Not that 'time' has any real relevance to the chapter itself, but I like to paint the whole picture.

And normally, I'm on point with seamlessly sewing the topics together. But in this instance, I have no 'neat way' of connecting the two segments. They are unsegmented. Like, you know... a lot of my life.

So instead of awkwardly forcing them together, like an uncomfortable introduction between good old Uncle Joe and literally anyone under twenty-one, I'm just gonna toss in this nonsensical little interlude and let it gloss over the poor transition.

You're welcome.

I do try to teach my kids about fitting in, whilst not losing themselves. About slotting into society, without becoming a zombie to the system.

And I think, at least some of that wisdom filters through to the right department. Case in point, a week or so ago, my *socially-awkward* but *desperate-for-a-hang-out-buddies* daughter asked my *socially-unaware* but *brilliantly-outgoing* son, *"How do you make friends? You just… do it. You make it look so simple!"*

Now, to add a bit of context here, my son's definition of a *friend* is someone he met at least thirty seconds ago at soft play or trampolining, and has already plunged headfirst into an unspoken game of chase with. And a *best friend*? That's someone with a name, a t-shirt colour, and a beaming smile, which he thinks is '*Soooo cute!*'

I love how simple things are for him.
How pure and uncomplicated it all feels.

Anyway, his response to his big sister? *"You just go up to them and say 'Hi'. And if they say hi back, then you play together and become friends!"*

Honestly, the simplicity of it is brilliant. The raw, unfiltered logic of just *asking*! No overthinking, no social awkwardness, no fear of rejection. Just *Hi*.

Of course, my almost teenage daughter slammed the idea in a matter of seconds. But she did it in the sweetest way, saying it wouldn't work for her as she doesn't have his '*charm*'. Her spirit animal would also likely be a sloth, or I'm thinking, maybe a black bear? Leave her alone and she'll just get on with life. Try and interfere, and she'll huff aggressively, initiate an impressive standoff, and then run away into the wilderness… of her room.

She and I would happily hibernate away from humanity, only venturing out for food and beach walks. We don't need forced small talk or unnecessary social interactions. Just a safe space, filled with hot chocolate, homemade brownies, and a mutual understanding that beyond our family, people-ing is overrated.

However, while she may be pretty unresponsive for much of the day, my daughter is prone to laughing *uncontrollably* at all my inappropriate jokes… Even the dark ones, like the time I said she'd be perfect for working in a morgue. I can't remember how that particular conversation spiralled, but I joked about how there'd be *"No awkward small talk, and if someone did strike up a conversation, it'd probably be a decapitated soul asking where their body went."*

Now you'd likely expect her to be modified. To squirm in uncomfortableness. And vow to disown me for suggesting such a thing. But this is my daughter. And so, without missing a beat, she glanced toward the imaginary cold slab across the room, pointed at it, and delivered, with full deadpan brilliance, *"Try over there, mate."*

I was creased.
Nearly spat my coffee out.
She's my absolute hero.
And my best friend.

We comment on things in unison, like two awkward minds sharing the same offbeat brainwave. We jab each other in the ribs, react with *stabby hands* of revenge, and then immediately fall about laughing, horrified at ourselves, but loving every ridiculous second of it.

We find comfort in each other's awkwardness. And in our solidarity to protect, nurture, and love my son. Because that's what being involved in someone's life should look like - mutual, supportive, and, in our case, filled with questionable humour and stabby hands of affection.

In true social media voice-over style... 'A few days later'... Because I, an almost certain, but not yet diagnosed, ADHDer living in a house full of shiny distractions, got, well, distracted, and started doing something else. My bad.

But I'm here now, full of the joys of 8:36am, having had approximately three hours' sleep.

"Why?" you ask, in some kind of subliminal message. Well, my son is full of cold and general blurghness. I know this because he spent most of yesterday lying out on the sofa, *which never happens.* Yes, he went to bed OK, but then woke up and cried through to me that his nose felt like it was going to explode.

It wasn't. I'm certain of that. But he did need Mama cuddles. And I will never deny them.

So we're running on sweet-smelling fumes today. And desperately trying to get this chapter finished before I curl up in a sloth-like position on the sofa until dawn.

It's always baffled me how some people seem to think *their* self-appointed involvement in our lives is, in some way, warranted. As a time-served home-edder, the biggest assumption I've found do-gooders make is that my kids will grow up to be antisocial reprobates with no future and zero chance in life. And that's down to my apparently selfish hippy lifestyle choices. My desperation to prove the world wrong. My inability to see the bigger picture and allow my kids to have a formal education with other young people… (*OK, technically that was more than one assumption, but let's not get caught up in details!)*

Newsflash - my daughter is already antisocial!

She gets that partly from me, and partly from her social anxiety shadows. Throwing her to the wolves, aka a 2000-kid packed school with high bullying rates and low support network, is not going to fix that. In fact, it will undoubtedly make it worse.

But I can assure you, neither she nor her brother will follow through with the reprobate suggestion. And they will have every opportunity to grow and follow their own paths to success.

My son wants to be… hang on, let me try and remember this…

- A piano teacher for children, *like him,* on a Monday and Tuesday.
- Work for his Mama on a Wednesday and Thursday.
- And do something space-related on Friday! This used to be '*travel into space'* until he realised *'space'* isn't a 9-5 gig. Turns out, months away from home wasn't his *'thing'*, so he revoked his astronaut application pronto!

Joking aside, and as cliché *(or far-fetched)* as they may be, I do want them both to follow their dreams. And I don't want my son's extra needs to make him feel like he can't.

But how do you stop that from happening?
How do I remove the barriers and let him see the open road ahead?

Right now, I smooth out the edges of his world before he even feels the bumps. I buy better spoons so eating cereal doesn't feel like a struggle. I keep him in Ninja pull-ups so incontinence doesn't dent his confidence.

Photo of the spoon triumph because this was literally life-changing for my kid! I get that sounds dramatic, which is, you know, so out of character for me. But that extra deep scoop-ability is the difference between my son eating and giving up out of 9am frustration.

And just in case you're wondering or in need, they're called kids' soup spoons!

I take him trampolining when other kids are at school, so he can bounce without anyone *breaking the rules* and jumping into his space. And I lay out his clean clothes in manageable groups because one big overwhelming pile might as well be a mountain, which he's just not able to climb.

He doesn't always notice these things, and I'm glad. His world feels just manageable enough without him seeing the scaffolding I've built around him. But I don't know what that will look like as he grows up.

And that plays heavily on my mind.

Of course, I will be there for as long as life allows me, running *(or, let's be real, later pottering in orthopaedic sneakers)* ten steps ahead to disarm any potential life-bombs. And if anyone dares suggest I shouldn't be, I will knock them into next Tuesday with my freakishly strong left hook.

(I don't know why my left arm is stronger. I assume some past-life nonsense where I was either a medieval jouster or a pub brawler with anger issues. Either way, call me Mama Bear Von Facepunch and know that I come armed with snacks and emotionally charged muscle memory!)

But don't worry - my fists of maternal fury are currently on sabbatical.

Today, we're swooning on the sofa. Wrapped in the kind of blankets that make life feel just a little less demanding. Munching on goodies, half for comfort, half for survival.

We're riding the waves of exhaustion, letting the quiet settle, and pretending that dozing off mid-sentence is just part of the vibe.

Peopling is officially out.
Cuddles are in.

And this chapter? This chapter is done, wrapped up in crumbs, chaos, and the soft hum of a day survived together.

Chapter 13: No Offence, But...

Social niceties
and other ridiculous lies.

"How bad is it? Run over a slug bad, or exploded badger bad?"

I won't tell you the run-up to that statement - it's more fun to let your mind be boggled. But trust me when I say, my son was somewhat amused by the carnage he had created. And of course, with my rateable scale of slugs vs badgers.

I do that a lot, use metaphors and analogies. You're probably thinking it's because my son, like many neurodiverse kids, needs visuals to make sense of this oh so confusing world, which is, erm... absolutely right!

Actually, no. That would be a logical and noble reason.

Plot twist - it's just way more fun. For them. For me. And for any unfortunate eavesdropper who happens to catch a whiff of my *"Why, after breakfast, did the floor look like a seagull had eaten too much yogurt, and then let nature take its course?"* mother-son speech.

I say mother-son, but I don't limit it just to my emotionally charged ostrich. Oh no. Just recently, I walked into my daughter's bedroom to find her laptop precariously balanced on the edge of her desk with a pint of juice not three inches away.

Not a big deal, you might think, however, I have the demonique twins, aka the cats, who wouldn't think twice about hurtling over said laptop and into the juice.

My words to the tech-reaper near-teen?

"Do you want your laptop to go fizzy fizzy pop pop bang bang gone?" to which she fell about laughing, asked me to repeat it, and then thankfully, granted her computer a last-minute pardon from certain death.

There was also the time when she dropped an entire container of metallic bag ties across my floor. And on walking in on said incident, I asked her, *"Did a unicorn throw up on my floor? Or is this an explosion of your questionable life choices and poor grip strength?"*

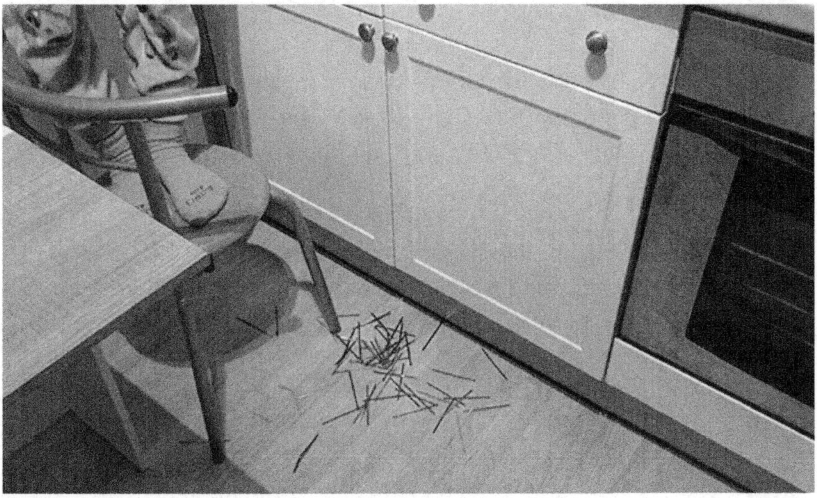

Some might say, *"It's all fun and games until someone takes it to heart"*. But don't worry - my kids are well-versed in my language of love and sarcasm. And they're even learning how to throw it right back at me, with just enough sass for me to choke on my coffee.

Does that make me a model parent?
Should I be applauded for raising offspring who dare to be mildly rude in jest while I do nothing but laugh it off?

No, probably not.

By some standards, I should be wielding a thousand broom handles, demanding apologies and providing only stale pancakes with lukewarm tap water. But instead, I choose to embrace the crazies, encourage my normally do-gooders to find their feet, test the boundaries, and understand the fine line between Mum-banter and, say, the post office queue or a neighbourhood fundraiser.

The problem only really arises when my son, a generally literal thinker, misses the joke and takes umbrage with statements like, *"Do you actually want to lose your skin? To be a tendon dangling weirdo who scares away old grannies?"*

Yes, I said that, when he shoved his hand not an inch below a pan from which I was serving up. And his response? *"No, of course not! Why would you say such a thing? I would get bacterians without skin. And blood would get in my bed!"*

See, he isn't exactly the most safety-conscious being. My boy rarely sees the danger, usually too blinkered by his own hurried thoughts. But I do my best, my real, messy, hold-it-all-together kind of best, to stay one step ahead of his spontaneous antics. The only problem is, my best doesn't come with a filter option.

I don't mean in a sweary, scare the begoblins out of him kind of way. No, it's more of a graphic, stop you in your tracks, what did she just say moment, which *can* get a few raised eyebrows when we're out.

Yes, people are naturally curious, judgmental, bewildered... I don't know, maybe just lacking a hobby? Which is fine, but the side glances, the passive-aggressive tutting, and the occasional self-important interruption, as if we're on some kind of reality show where strangers feel entitled to cast their votes on our parenting, can be tough to swallow. It's as if they believe they've been appointed the Simon Cowell of public behaviour, ready to offer their unsolicited critique with all the grace of a hippo on roller skates.

One of my most memorable *'public parenting reviews'* happened last year on a Wednesday evening trip to ASDA. My daughter was in drama club. And so, it was my son and I who were galloping through the fruit and veg aisles, as though it was made of cotton candy and giggle gas.

Now, for those in the know, he, like a few other sensory-led children I know, will only accept fruit in its most liquid form, aka baby pouches. Of course, we don't *call* them baby pouches - my son is not a baby. My baby, yes, but not an actual baby. His eating habits, on the other hand, can, at times, still resemble that of a cranky, just-woke-up-from-a-nap two-year-old who refuses to eat anything that isn't smooth, conveniently packaged, and delivered with the ease of a squeeze.

Offer him a strawberry? No chance.
A banana? Absolutely not.
Blueberries? Don't make me laugh.

But puree those bad boys down, stick them in a brightly coloured squeezy pouch, and suddenly, we're in 5-a-day business.

I should start writing ads for these sensory-friendly companies! Ease of a squeeze? Puree those bad boys down? That's pure marketing gold!

Anyway, on this particular pouch dash, I had no idea we were about to be assessed by yet another self-appointed expert in child-rearing.

As I guided my emotionally charged ostrich through the grand decision of selecting five boxes of fruit mush, a woman, cradling a one(ish)-year-old on her hip, gave me a knowing nod and said,

"Oh, you're just like us! We have to buy them like that too. How old is your little one?"

To which I replied, *“He's eight... Years. He's eight years old, and this is the only way to get fruit down him.”*

And I swear to you, I watched this woman's face go through the five stages of grief in real-time.

1. Confusion.
2. Shock.
3. Denial.
4. Bargaining *(with herself, probably)*.
5. And finally, disgust.

Now, this would be the part where most people feel the need to justify themselves. Explain the autism. The sensory issues. The fact that *'real'* fruit might as well be served with a side of live slugs for all the good it'll do. But no. I wasn't in the mood for educational outreach. My shopping trolley didn't require a press release. So instead, I just grinned, turned my trolley a full 180', and started to walk away.

And then, with the comedic timing of an absolute *pro*, my son turned to her and cheerfully chirped, *'Have a nice day!'* - a phrase I've taught him to say when leaving people. And it honestly couldn't have been better timed.

"Start stripping before I start whipping!" I just called across the hallway.

That's practically a classic in my parenting repertoire, a phrase that rolls off the tongue on autopilot whenever my son is taking his sweet time getting ready for a bath. But today? Today, I heard it back in real-time and realised... wow. That does *not* sound great out of context.

Cue my son collapsing into fits of giggles while I stand there, facepalming at my own life choices. Because let's be real, anyone overhearing this would assume I run a household that requires a safe word.

For clarity, I do *not* whip my children. That's both illegal and frowned upon in most social circles. But I do playfully threaten them, because that's just the brand of chaotic parenting we thrive on, much like my infamous, "I'll rip your arm off and slap you with the soggy end" saga, which, despite sounding like a WWE promo gone wrong, has proven oddly effective at getting my kids to stop dawdling.

One day, he's going to casually drop these lines in front of some well-meaning stranger – probably a cashier, a doctor, or, worse, the *nosy neighbour* who already looks at me like I might be harbouring criminal tendencies.

Oh well. C'est la vie!

I feel that much of society seems to have plummeted headfirst down some dark rabbit hole and landed in a never-ending game of *'Snowflake vs. Karen!'* In my head *(a scary place I know!)* it's like Twister, but with extra entitlement, where someone's foot is always lodged firmly in someone else's butt. And each spin of the board produces a brand-new reason to be mortally offended.

They are both, simultaneously, the victim and the prosecutor. As individuals and as a clam *(yes, a clam, because they do tend to group together and clamp down hard on anything that doesn't fit their narrative),* they demand change, but only of others.

They want equality, but with extra perks just for them.
They cry for acceptance, but without the need to accept anyone else.
And above all, they insist on their right to voice their unhappiness.

But if you dare do the same? Well, congratulations, you're now toxic, problematic, or, worse… *one of them!* I swear, with every fresh outrage, the bar gets lowered. And one day, we'll likely be watching a full-blown socially-streamed war over whether blinkers on cars are a microaggression against the directionally challenged.

I get it. We all pass judgment, with or without meaning to. I try to internalise mine. Or, at least whisper very quietly, so as not to offend the poor soul whose life decisions really needed to slap them round the face this morning. And I try to teach the kids the same. Sure, some situations might seem odd to us, kooky, even uncomfortable. But unless someone is actively endangering lives, the world could do with a little contrast now and then. I mean, they have to put up with me. That's their normal.

But watching the world put up with me? That's a whole different experience. My daughter, in particular, has long clocked the awkward stares at my body armour of ink. The unimpressed huffs at my children daring to exist outside of a school building. The appalled jaw drops when I loudly proclaim that "*Vegetables' lives matter too!*" in a predominantly vegan gathering…

For the record, I'm not anti-vegan. Food is food.

I'm just anti-vegans who judge me for eating a bacon and egg sandwich at lunch, or worse, try to traumatise my kids with stories about baby chicks watching their mothers die, just so I can enjoy a Sunday roast in peace - wWe don't need that kind of emotional manipulation before dessert, thank you very much.

As with anything in life, it's your choice to make. And I fully respect your decision, in that it's not mine, I don't have to live by it, and I sure as heck don't need to pretend a roasted cauliflower is in any way comparable to the deeply spiritual experience that is gravy-drenched meat and potatoes.

You live your truth.
I'll live mine (preferably with stuffing, roasties, and zero judgement from Brenda with the quinoa breath!)

Gravy, anyone?

Funny story… or at least it might've been, if it wasn't now 10:45pm and I'd only just curled up on the sofa with my laptop. But given my current *"Who am I to judge?"* ramblings, the last two hours feel oddly fitting.

Around 9:45pm, I was doing the usual half-hearted bedtime chase. Yes, I know - that's late. Kids need their sleep, blah blah blah. But timekeeping isn't exactly my strong suit, and I had very little motivation to unsnuggle them.

Anyway, my boy then appeared. Sheepish expression. Hands tucked behind his back.

"I have no pull-ups left," he mumbled. So I ran upstairs to check. And his drawer was, in fact, a barren wasteland of unmet bladder security. Not a pull-up in sight. Panic obviously set in. I asked my daughter to raid my bag, and she found but one lonely pull-up. My options were… Well, there weren't any. A trip to Tesco was needed. And my eagerness for the adventure, yeah, it was somewhat lacking.

As I bundled the kids into a slightly frozen car (it was -1°C tonight!), I could tell something was off with my boy. There was that look. Not a full-on tragic episode of *EastEnders* kind of look, but definitely more than a casual *"Meh."* So I gently asked what was up.

Turned out, he was feeling guilty for not telling me sooner that his pull-up stash had run low. And honestly, I got it. I felt bad too, like a kick in the stomach bad. I should never have expected him to keep track in the first place. That was a big ask.

Self-pity aside, I reassured him it was no big deal. Tesco was only fifteen minutes away, and he'd be back in bed soon, tucked up with Fred Ted, Colin the Cow, and Si-Si.

FYI, Si-Si is a rabbit I bought him before he was even born. It was meant to be called Lucy, but he could never pronounce it. Also, and this is entirely my own doing, Si-Si is now a triplet, thanks to my unhealthy habit of popping into IKEA when he was little. My boy would get upset seeing 'his rabbit' in the giant teddy mountain, convinced it had somehow escaped. So yes... I bought a new one every single time. I regret nothing.

Now, what was actually fitting about the whole *Tesco-dash* situation was the unofficial underground car meet-up that was going on in the store car park. Maybe eight or ten Fords and Vauxhalls, with engines revving, exhausts growling, and neon lights flickering like they were summoning Fast & Furious energy in aisle seven.

It took me right back to my teenage years, riding shotgun in my incredibly cool boyfriend's Escort, convoying through town, feeling effortlessly cool. The year 2000, I think. A lifetime ago.

But my kids, especially my daughter, were shocked that Tesco allowed the *reprobates (her current favourite word, not because she has some deep connection with the tribe; she just likes how the word sounds)* to hang out at the bottom of the car park. That they were probably putting shoppers off; that they looked intimidating, and the security guards should probably *do their job (again, her words)* and come move them on.

She's a fretter, my kid.
A worrier among warriors.

But we chatted it out on the drive home, and I explained how most of them are harmless car enthusiasts, geeking out over engines, enjoying the acoustics of the concrete ceilings. About how they probably have licenses *(hopefully!)*, but no real idea how to drive. I mean, they can obviously drive, but not *drive*... And then, to lighten the mood, I floored it just enough to make her laugh.

Oh, and Tesco had a ridiculous Clubcard deal on a giant tub of Heroes, which was too good to miss. Watching my son light up as I let him pick three on the drive home? Worth every second of the freezing late-night trek.

I guess it's human nature to jump to conclusions. I, for one, love making up ridiculous backstories for random strangers.

"You see the rubbish collector? He used to be in a high-end job, something in management, but the stress got so bad.
His marriage was on the rocks, his health about to give out.
So one day, he just got up and quit. And found this job, cleaning the paths and emptying bins.
And is now carefree, whistling away to himself in the sun."

But, unless they happen to waltz into my life armed with rudeness and an overinflated sense of self-importance, I'll happily keep those stories to myself. I mean, I'm not here to upset folk *(yes, I heard that sputter of drink… This whole book is built on inappropriate and likely offensive remarks… But not the personal type. I just want to bring a little joy, a little laughter when you know you shouldn't, and a little sense of 'I feel that too!')*

Should people choose to grace my world with unsolicited superiority, however, well… that's an entirely different beast altogether.

For that, I shall metaphorically dismantle them, piece by pretentious piece, like an architect of poetic justice.
I shall tear down their ivory tower, brick by self-righteous brick.
And cast them into the gutter, where their only supper shall be cold fish bones and the bitter taste of their own misplaced opinions!

That little moment amused me far more than it should have!

Honestly, I'm now thinking my next book should be some epic, heroic, dragon-slaying tale of parenthood, complete with fire-breathing, orange-furred morons (a title I regularly bestow upon the youngest cat) and a brigade of French-bobbed feminists, hell-bent on world domination.

Or, maybe not. I don't think it would sell particularly well.

Not that I'm convinced *this* book will either, but hey, I cling to hope the same way I cling to my sanity – desperately, while drowning in an emotional sea of caffeine and cake.

Moving on...

To the man who turned a blind eye when your son laughed at mine for carrying his teddy around ASDA, I saw you. I saw you give that sideways glance and *choose not* to teach your kid to do better.

To the woman who tutted at the park when my kids were playing out in the fresh air at 12:30pm on a Thursday afternoon, I heard you. I heard you mutter that it was a disgrace, that they should be in school. But you didn't think to ask, did you? Or better still, enjoy their laughter under the sun rather than try to rain on my parade.

And to the Mum who breaks her heart, when her child can't toilet train, like every other kid you know. Won't eat with the family, like other kids you know. And can't understand why no one wants to play in the park with them, and instead calls them *weird* or *stupid*… I feel you. I feel your pain, your worry, your heartache, and sleepless nights.

Because at the end of the day, we all look. We all watch the world around us with curiosity, with judgment, with assumptions. But what we *choose* to do with that moment of observation? That's on us.

We can choose kindness.
We can choose understanding.
Or we can choose to mind our own damn business.
We can choose to offer a smile instead of a glare.
A nod instead of a sigh.
A *"Hey, you're doing great"* instead of a whispered judgment.
We can choose to extend patience instead of rolling our eyes.
To ask instead of assume.
To uplift instead of tear down…

And I can choose to ignore the intrusive thoughts that are nagging me to mow down the sanctimonious sausage-rolls who waddle through life, dispensing judgment like it's buy-one-get-one-free at the hypocrisy counter.

Because the only thing worse than their unsolicited advice is the fact that they think it's a public service.

Spoiler alert: it's not.
It's emotional littering.
And I'm not picking it up.

Side note: *I've officially spent more money on puréed fruit pouches than I did on my first car. And honestly? The pouches are more reliable. They don't leak oil, argue back, or fail their MOT. They just sit quietly in the cupboard, full of vitamins and false hope.*

Chapter 14: He's A Limited Edition

Polite(ish) ways to say
"Kindly Shove It!"

Unsolicited parenting advice? I'll take a double-shot, please.

You know, that charming, uninvited commentary that drifts in like a passive-aggressive genie, summoned not by a magic lamp, but by the simple act of your child existing a little differently in public. It's infuriating. Somewhat degrading. And on days when my people skills have packed up and left without notice, it can be highly offensive.

Honestly, it's a mid-March miracle that I've made it this far, without aggressively throwing a fidget spinner at someone's forehead. Believe me, I've thought about it. Often. With impressive aim. But unfortunately, prison food is neither appealing nor allergy-friendly.

Besides, I've already got my hands full. Raising a neurodiverse child comes with a daily to-do list that feels like it was drafted by Uncle Tod right after getting slapped with a speeding ticket in Torquay and realising his online date was actually his second cousin.

It's bitter. It's personal. And it reads like it was written by a man who's one lukewarm latte away from a full-blown breakdown. That's the kind of chaos we're working with.

So no, I don't need the village idiot piping up to tell me my child's *'misbehaviour'* is due to an unbalanced aura. Nor do I need someone who once raised a pet goldfish explaining how *"a firm bedtime and less iPad time"* will magically solve everything.

And yet, they still come. Like unsolicited flyers, or parking attendants in a red light district. The stray irritants.

So this chapter?

I offer it as a toolkit. A sarcasm-laced survival guide for those moments when someone decides *you* need *their* opinion. You don't. But let's prepare anyway, with twenty comebacks for unsolicited advice that you'll likely struggle to say with a straight face.

1. "He doesn't look autistic."
"Yeah, we sent him back and asked for the limited-edition model with invisible traits. So glad you noticed."

2. "All kids do that."
"Absolutely. And all adults say unhelpful things. Isn't it wild how common it is?"

3. "You just need to be stricter with discipline."
"Right, because nothing soothes a sensory meltdown like a good old-fashioned power trip. Shall I get my Victorian parenting manual out?"

4. "He'll grow out of it."
"Perfect. While we're at it, I'm hoping I'll grow out of being exhausted and judged in public. Fingers crossed!"

5. "Maybe you should try this therapy I read about."
"Brilliant. While we're trading miracle cures, I've got this amazing seaweed smoothie that cures unsolicited advice. Want the recipe?"

6. "Is he on medication? You should consider it."
"He's not, but I might be soon. You know, just to cope with conversations like this one."

7. "Are you sure he has autism? He seems fine to me."
"Oh thank goodness you said that! I was worried the multiple professional assessments were wrong, but you've known him for a whole 47 seconds, so that's a relief."

8. "It's probably just a phase."
"Yes! We're currently in the 'neurodivergent with complex support needs' phase. Next up, according to your psychic insight, is the 'suddenly becomes neurotypical' phase. It should be any day now."

9. "Isn't ADHD just an excuse for bad behaviour?"
"Only if being born with a different brain structure counts as a cheeky little excuse. But sure, tell me more about your diploma in Not Knowing What You're Talking About. I'd love to hear all about it!"

10. "You should be grateful it's not something worse."
"You're right. I should be grateful it's just the daily emotional Olympics, regular battles with systems that don't work, and absolutely zero sleep. What a breeze!"

11. "She'll eat when she's hungry enough."
"Brilliant advice. I'll just tell her sensory system to stop being dramatic and enjoy the delightful texture of slightly wet broccoli. Problem solved."

12. "There was none of this malarky in my day!"
"No, in your day they just called it being 'naughty', smacked it out of you, and sent everyone to therapy 40 years later. A simpler time."

13. "There's a name for everything now!"
"Yes! It's wild. Apparently 'being a judgemental nightmare' still doesn't have one though. Tragic oversight."

14. "Is it because his Dad isn't around?"
"Oh absolutely. Neurodevelopmental conditions are well-known for being emotionally offended by family structures. Autism took one look at our situation and went, 'Yep, moving in.'"

15. "Maybe, if you put him in school, rather than this home educated nonsense, he'd settle down."
"Ah yes, nothing says calm and regulated like 30 kids, fluorescent lights, and a rotating supply teacher shouting about phonics. But don't worry, our 'nonsense' includes actual learning. And snacks. Lots of snacks."

16. "Are you one of those Munchausen syndrome by proxy parents? I've heard of them."
"Oh yes. I just adore filling in endless forms, battling systems for basic support, and crying into paperwork. So glamorous. You should try it - it's like getting high, but with no sleep and you kind of notice the judgment."

17. "You shouldn't label him - it'll hold him back."
"Right, let's just go with 'mysterious chaos child', guess his needs based on his current 'vibes' and hope for the best.

18. *"I'm guessing you claim all sorts? A right money maker!"*
"Absolutely! Between sensory chews, 7 loads of washing a day, and educational resources, I'm practically knee-deep in gold glue sticks. Champagne 'n' meltdowns, darling - it's a lifestyle."

19. *"Kids like that just need more exercise."*
"Great idea. I'll swap pencil work and baking with mama for a military style bootcamp. Maybe if he sprints for 12 hours straight, he'll stop being autistic and eat Porridge Oats. Win-win!"

20. *"You're making a big deal out of nothing."*
"You're right. I'll just quietly ignore every meltdown, system failure, and sleepless night while pretending we're thriving. Want to borrow my cape, or is gaslighting your superpower already?"

So there you go. Twenty solid comebacks, pre-loaded and ready to deploy the next time someone mistakes your life for a community suggestion box.

Will you actually say any of them out loud? Probably not. Most of us are too tired, too polite, or too busy trying to stop our kids from licking who knows what. But *thinking* them? *Imagining* them landing like a glitter bomb in the middle of an unsolicited opinion buffet? That, my friend, is self-care.

Because when you can't wield a baseball bat, humour is the next best thing. And unlike a baseball bat, it's socially acceptable, legal, and doesn't require you to mop up afterwards.

You're welcome.

Notes From the Edge

3rd March 2025 ♡

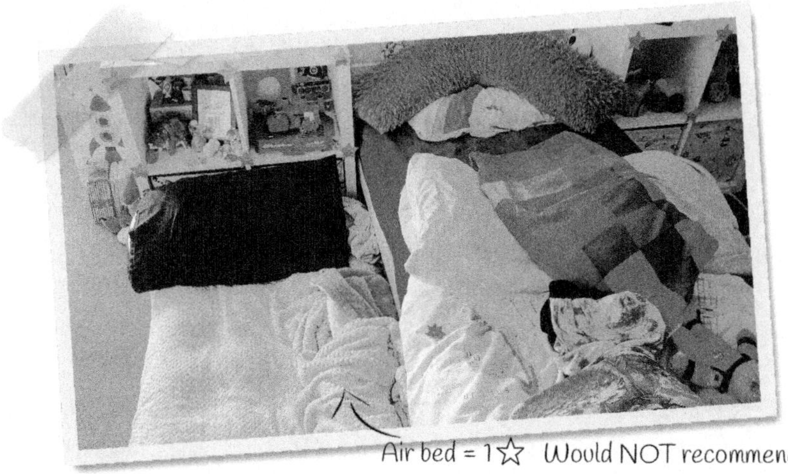

Air bed = 1☆ Would NOT recommend!

To the pheasant I accidentally hit in the car last week, I think I finally understand your pain. I feel your innermost misery, the aches, the disorientation. And I'm sorry... Although you did CHOOSE to run out in front of my car, and my options were sort of limited at 60mph!

But still. I'm almost certain that my current state of unwellness is on par with your narrowly escaped 'flapping ghost of the tarmac' incident. I just hope your headache (aka the concussion felt from my car bumper) was gentler than the intermittent migraines I've been experiencing for the past few days. And that your bladder control is somewhat more reliable than mine has been during these, what can only be described as, violent sneezing episodes (though, I can totally appreciate that it probably wouldn't be, in the moments prior to your near-death experience!)

Yes. I think that's well and truly set the tone for this chapter!

It's Monday again. No music, again (due to lurgies and Mr D not wanting them, which is kind of understandable!) ♬⋆.˚

And I'm running on what feels like seventeen minutes of sleep, spread over four long, child-temperature-spiking, tear-flowing, snot-bubbling nights. Two of which I've spent on the air bed next to my son, primed and ready to launch at the first sign of hallucinating night terrors, and/or 6am nose explosions ⋆✴︎˚｡⋆

I honestly don't know how to person today. I am so full of this flu-like virus, yet still trying to function on some level. Because, well, motherhood stops for no one.

What's that saying? I don't have time to be ill. I really don't. But if you feel like whipping out your miniature violin and a box of extra soft tissues, that would be amazing!

Anyway... I did bake homemade cheese scones for lunch. That was my epic parenting moment of the day. I also made my son cry for suggesting that he could write one sentence for learning time. In contrast, that was not my epic parenting moment of the day.

My eyeliner is a bleak smudge of yesterday's 'human being' efforts. My hair, now long enough to bun, is bunned. And the leggings that I vowed never to wear outside? I wore them out for the ten-minute errand I had to run. I honestly have zero ducks of shame left to give 🦢 But aside from my own 'could-be-middle-aged, could-be-fibromyalgia, could-be-flu-virus-lurgy' aches, I have to contend with my son, who's singing his own song of sufferance.

Now, three days ago, I would have undoubtedly blamed Manful for his angst with the world. He was at one with the sniffles and the blurghness. But now? Now we are just brimming with self-pity and general wrongness.

This morning, he sat at the kitchen table and endured at least eight minutes of soggy cereal woefulness. Unlike most mornings, he was sat on his own, what with his sister sleeping off a rough night and me, doing, I can't remember what 🌀 And the lack of people on hand to pick up on his dramatic huffing and puffing only seemed to worsen the inadequate breakfast offerings.

Strike one.

The follow-up bawling was brought to us by Frankie, my orange-flavoured half-wit. He chose today of all days to put on a hilarious performance of 'The Bengal, The Witch, and The Wardrobe' as my already grumbling son went to pick out a fresh t-shirt for the day.

Apparently, the cat's jumping in and 'ignoring' my child's demands to 'leave the wardrobe now' only added to his already bothersome morning. And it did, in fact, result in a further six minutes of grunting and groaning, before I gave in and called him down to reenact the show... Or rather, that's what he did when asked what the problem was.

Strike two.

It was not going well. And after realizing we had unintentionally dodged almost all 'learning time' over the past five days of illness, I, the mother of all fluff ups, managed to exacerbate the already direful state of affairs by calling upon my now dressed and (at that point) slightly less grumbly child to fetch his letter game from up in my office.

Now, it's a big, bright box. It's new, so it should register high on his radar. It's in plain sight, mainly because it won't fit anywhere else. And on any other day, it would have been an easy grab-and-go situation. A takeaway with no queue. A self-service without the annoying 'Please place your item on the scale' for the seventh time.

Only that day was not today.

No. Despite the very clear, very obvious instructions on where to locate the fantastical game, my child did little more than sit in the middle of my office floor, throwing his head around in a rollercoaster ride motion, shrieking the words, "Where? Where? I can't see it!" fifteen times.

Did I unwittingly forget where I'd put the box?
Did I move it without thinking?
Did I accidentally sell it with the hobbits and misplace the three silver pennies they'd paid me in return?

No. My child was just in 'that' mood. And even with flashing lights, a fluff off big arrow, and a flock of dancing Cockatoos to show the way, he would have still sat there in denial that the box ever existed.

Strike three. And we're out ☠

I'm done with today. My fuzzy head reminds me of a hangover from the early 2000s... Not a place I want to go back to. And my person skills have been shipped off, along with my Amazon return box.

There is, however, the somewhat humbling smell of a chicken casserole consuming the house. I threw it in the slow cooker a couple of hours ago, whilst I still had some ducks to give. And knowing that comfort food shall be on the table soon warms my soul a few degrees... or that might just be my recurring temperature spike. Who knows!

I am also thankful that no school runs shall take place, not now in the midst of this illness, not ever. The thought of standing at the prison fence... I mean school gate... with a bunch of people I have no wish to share oxygen with, sends shivers down my spine. I've done it before, I know the drill.

And I'd rather write an awkward twenty-nine-verse poem on mushrooms than go back there again. Why twenty-nine? Because it will feel incomplete. 'Tis neither a four-beat twenty-eighter, nor a rounded-up thirty-er. And that's just wrong. Almost as wrong as eating mushrooms. Little fungus houses. Yuck!

So here's to home-education, and the win against any school gate shams. Here's to avoiding people and using my lurgy as an imaginary lightsaber against the crowds. And here's to feeling better, to sleeping for more than twenty consecutive minutes. And to my emotionally charged ostrich, not battling the orange-flavoured cat for wardrobe rights.

Honestly, you couldn't write this stuff.
Oh wait. I am!

> "Mothers talk about sleep the way someone who is starving talks about food." - Kathleen Kendall-Tackett, Ph.D

Chapter 15: So That's Illegal

Big sister energy.
Bigger shovel energy.

We were driving home from the beach a few days ago, windswept, tired, and thoroughly arcade'd out. And out of nowhere, one of the weirdest conversations started brewing between my kids in the backseats.

Daughter *(casually, but with a dramatic flair): "I best be invited to your wedding when you're older."*
Son: *"Well… maybe. I don't know yet."*
Daughter: *"What do you mean you don't know?! I need to be there! I'm your sister!"*
Son *(serious face, matter-of-fact tone): "Isn't it illegal to marry your sister?"*

Now, had I been drinking a cuppa or diving headfirst into a much-needed slice of cake at the time, I think I might have choked at his response. But thankfully, I wasn't.

And even more thankfully, my daughter jumped in before I could say a word, eyes wide, laughing in horror,

"Yes! Absolutely yes, it's illegal! But I didn't mean that! I meant when you marry someone else, I want to be there. Like… as a guest!"

Son: *"That's okay then. Because I'm pretty sure marrying your actual sister is a crime."*
Daughter: *"It is. But I just want to come to your wedding, not star in it!"*
Son: *"Ok. So when I marry a different girl, not you, someone else, you can be there. But not in a marrying way."*

With sudden seriousness, my daughter nodded. *"Great. And if she ever hurts you… like, breaks your heart? I'll dispose of the body."*
And it was at this point, while trying to park, that I felt the need to step in, you know, as the supposed responsible parent in the room.

Me: *"I'm sorry, what?! How did we get from wedding invites to murder?!"*
Daughter *(laughing wildly): "I don't know! It escalated quickly!"*
Me *(trying my best to keep a straight face): "What your sister means is… We'll always protect you. We'll always be there."*
Daughter *(completely deadpan): "And get rid of the body!"*

I didn't know whether to be proud of her loyalty or mildly traumatised that *this* was her go-to. Not that I'm worried she's headed down the serial-stabber route - she's far too antisocial to join a cult, let alone start one.

I just wonder what the actual heckerty-hoo-ha she's watching on YouTube. And, more inappropriately… if it's worth searching up for a Friday night crime fest!

Me *(without thinking): "You'll need pigs for that. Pigs eat everything."*
Daughter: *"Yes! We'll raise piglets. No one will ever know."*
Me: *"Well, just make sure you get rid of the belt buckles. Pigs don't eat metal."*
Daughter *(without missing a beat): "That's fine. We'll take anything of value to the pawn shop."*
Me *(almost tripping over my own dropped jaw): "I'm sorry - how do you even know what a pawn shop is?!"*

She just shrugged.
Like it was common knowledge.
Like every near-teen girl had a secret plan involving pig disposal, belt buckles, and offloading valuables for cash.
You know… just in case.

And yeah, it was funny. Hilarious, actually. But underneath the madness, there's this thing she's always had. This fierce, automatic need to protect her brother.

It's not loud or dramatic. It's just in the way she watches him. The way she steps in before I even have to ask.

She's been like that since he was a baby. Not right from day one - those newborn days were rough. She was only four at the time *(and a bit - she'd insist on that part),* and suddenly she wasn't the baby anymore. She didn't know where she fit. And I think she was hurt, watching someone else in my arms.

But that storm passed. Within a few months, she fell in love with him. And had this way of knowing what he needed. Like no one told her. She just knew.

When I got sick, with what I now believe was COVID, right at the start of the pandemic, my Mum was *'too busy'* to help. Milk, bread, and basic human decency were just too much effort. And so it was my daughter who kept things going. She was just seven years old, performing the most epic Mary Poppins recital, without even being asked.

She helped get him dressed, sorted snacks, managed the TV remote like it was a hostage negotiation, and gave me play-by-plays from the floor as I drifted in and out of consciousness on the sofa.

"Don't worry, Mum, he's got juice and I changed his nappy."

I felt awful. Proper stomach-knotting, heart-aching guilt. She should never have had to carry that kind of weight. But I could barely lift my head, let alone parent properly, for two and a half days. And she just... handled it.

I didn't have to ask her to step up.
She just did.
And still does.

She calms him when he's overwhelmed. Talks him down from his emotional cliffs and grabs his hand near actual ones, because he has zero spatial awareness, or any kind of impending danger alarm in his beautiful little mind.

They do still bicker, of course. They're siblings, not spiritual soulmates. Just last week, I walked in on a heated argument over the dusty cereal at the bottom of the box. My son has a long-term hatred for the debris, and my daughter knows this. But somehow, it still ended up in his bowl, for which she was almost certainly at fault.

He accused her, using his finest old-man-ranty tone, of *"ruining his breakfast",* which she counter-argued with *"you could have just left that part - it wouldn't have killed you".* And admittedly, both valid points, albeit not worthy of a full-scale kitchen floor standoff.

I just stood there in yesterday's leggings and bleach-stained hoodie, sipping my coffee like a work-experience marriage counsellor, quietly relieved. Because to me, these episodes mean she's not stuck in Big Sister Guardian Mode. I've always insisted that she's allowed to get annoyed when he reaches for her spoon *"because it's nice to share,"* or point out twenty times that she has paint on her arm, after claiming she'd already washed it off.

It's kind of beautiful, in a slightly deranged way. Their sibling dynamic isn't picture-perfect or plucked from a wholesome family drama. It's chaos and comfort tangled together like a roll of sellotape that's lost the end and now exists purely to test your will to live.

They drive each other up the wall, then hold each other when the world gets too loud. One minute they're arguing over who closed the door on whose toe, the next they're united in some tent-building exercise that spans my entire living room and leaves me chairless in the kitchen… apparently, they're structurally crucial to the whole camp vibe!

And me? I'm somewhere in the middle, breaking up debates over invisible boundaries, sweeping up cereal shrapnel like it's confetti after a war, and quietly reconsidering whether the piglet thing was a joke, a threat, or the launch of a highly illegal but weirdly well-branded family cartel.

Matching T-shirts.
Encrypted group chats.
A custom-built pig shed with CCTV.

Honestly, the way this household operates, I wouldn't even be surprised if there's a logo being designed as we speak. Probably by my daughter. Probably in GIMP *(her go-to online design tool, not a fashion choice… although, now that you mention it!)* And almost certainly in…

Blood Red Quintessential font!

(That line should have been printed in red ink, however, the cost of living affects us all. And grayscale was the only option that didn't require selling a kidney, or the naming rights to my future grandchildren!)

Chapter 16: He Isn't Broken

Sensory storms and sunshine days.
(Also, the kiwi started it!)

"I don't know why you just can't get your life together. You need to get things straight, stop messing everything up. It's like you need therapy, all this sad juice everywhere. Seriously, just get it together... kiwi!"

And no, my daughter wasn't talking about New Zealanders or the weird little birds. She was berating an actual piece of fruit, fully committed to a dramatic takedown of its nature and apparent mission to turn her lunch into a soggy catastrophe. And it was beyond comical to watch. My normally shy, somewhat reserved near-teen had transformed into an old biddy at the bus stop, rattling off her grievances, of the kiwi's refusal to be eaten without drenching her favorite jeans in sticky, green regret.

You see, it's usually my son who's rambling on about the obscene amount of reflective bollards needed on one junction *(yes, that happened today too!)* or demanding to know why the cats, primarily the orange moron, had to *destroy* his hanging window art.

Yes, overreactions are common in this house. Almost obligatory at times.

If my son is sad, even just the tiniest amount, the emotional floodgates will open. There will be tears, hysterical tears, and the world around comes crashing down. His small arms will be thrown around my neck with desperate urgency, his breathing sharp and uneven, and sometimes, the sobs will come so hard and fast that he's left gasping, struggling to find solid ground beneath the weight of it all.

That's a pretty standard response if and when he gets in trouble, not that it happens often. He's a gentle kid, usually trying to do right. But on the rare occasions when he does slip up, the reaction is so utterly devastating that to an outsider, it would look like something much darker.

You see, his sadness isn't just sadness. It's heartbreak, complete and overwhelming. The kind of despair you'd expect from a child who's been berated and broken down over the years, not one raised in love, kindness, and understanding.

I know how my son's upset might look. I know how easy it would be for someone to judge. And I get it. We've all seen the posters pinned to the back of public toilet doors; the leaflets in GP waiting rooms. The ones that tell you to '*watch for the quiet kids*', the ones who crumble under the weight of a mistake, because they're expecting punishment.

And at times, my child could fit that description. His emotional responses are extreme; his distress raw and unsettling to see. But the truth is miles apart from the warning signs printed in black and white.

> *He isn't afraid. He isn't broken.*
> *He just feels everything too much.*

He struggles to regulate and feels emotions at a level that the world doesn't consider *'normal.'*

I do sometimes wonder, if a stranger saw this moment, would they understand? Or would they assume the worst? And I know I'm not alone in this fear.

I've seen it echoed across social media, in the desperate pleas of parents searching for reassurance. Parents who lie awake at night, hearts pounding, wondering if today's public meltdown, the screaming, the flailing, the heartbreak that comes with dysregulation, was seen by the wrong person. If the 2am cries, the ones that shake the walls and rattle their exhausted bones, will summon the police, a concerned neighbour, or worse, social services.

Because the world doesn't always see neurodivergence for what it is. They don't see the love, the patience, the relentless devotion of parents and carers, trying to guide their children through an emotional storm they can't yet navigate.

No, they just see the noise, the chaos, the pieces that look on the surface, like something far more sinister. And that's terrifying.

Thankfully, for us, those moments are rarely in front of strangers. And all they tend to see is a Blue Smartie advert in full motion - spinning, running, high-pitched laughing… and, if they happen to linger long enough, a twenty-minute seminar on the seven colour-coded mats that came with our new chopping board. Either that or an ostrich-certified explanation of "*How a household fan works in a similar fashion to an everyday hoover*". Good old Echolalia and YouTube, working together in chaotic harmony!

Yes, we have good days and bad days, just like any other family. And that formidable benchmark? It's often set before my feet have even hit the ground. But we also have good moments, which can be high vault into bad ones.

Yup, my son can flip quicker than a pancake in a brand new non-stick pan - one second golden and perfect, the next, stuck to the ceiling while everyone panics. These wrecking ball-sized pendulums are almost always over something that you or I would consider small, trivial, close to igsignifactn…

I went to correct that, my inexplicably bad 'spelling' mistake... Can I even call it a spelling mistake? It's like a whole new language, made up entirely of brain farts and spaghetti rings! I think I'm tired. No,. I *know* I'm tired.

In...sig...nif...icant. Got there in the end!

Now, just for dramatic effect, I thought I'd list off ten things that sent my emotionally charged ostrich into a full-blown meltdown recently:

1. He was helping me hang laundry, only the T-shirt sleeve was inside out, and his single flick of the wrist did not, in fact, magically fix it.
2. Piano practice was going well… until Frankie, the orange-flavoured wildebeest, took a leisurely *stomp* across the keys, mid-play.
3. My son was hoovering the cat mats with the handheld vacuum, but the anti-litter-everywhere material was clinging onto the grains like a stubborn ex.

4. The pasta that he wanted, insisted he liked, and specifically requested, went cold. *Twice.* And was then rejected.
5. Three nappy bags came out of the packet instead of one. *Three.* This was an unacceptable act of defiance from the plastic gods.
6. The car smelled like a toaster having a midlife crisis, which was an alarming plot twist given the *warm* weather and lack of instant breeze factor, because, well, we were still parked up.
7. His sister spoke over him. *Twice.* Before 9:30am. The sheer audacity.
8. I failed to teleport a towel to his face in under three seconds during a recent shower. Unfit mother confirmed.
9. His tablet wasn't charged overnight because *he* didn't tell *me* it needed charging, and so it was left limping along at 3% like a wounded soldier.
10. I did not say *"Love you"* when leaving the bedroom to go to the bathroom, which, frankly, might be my greatest parenting failure to date.

I shouldn't laugh. I know. These things genuinely bother him in the moment, like an itch he just can't reach with. And his feelings? Completely valid. But... At what point do our kids, neurodiverse or otherwise, have that magical lightbulb moment and realize that sometimes, life just sucks? And understand that throwing a dramatic wobbler only turns minor suckiness into full-blown apocalypse vibes.

I want my boy to get that. To understand that yes, the carpet cleaner hose was annoyingly laid out in the bathroom, but it wasn't a personal attack - it was just in the way. Temporarily. Like a mild inconvenience with a handle.

To appreciate that, yes, I took *almost* two minutes to get to him during a pull-up changing crisis, but that doesn't mean I love him any less. It just means I was rescuing dinner from the hob so it didn't burn, and then trying not to trip over the orange-flavoured assassin on my way up the stairs.

Don't worry - the Frankster is very much alive, despite how this photo looks. He'd just worn himself out with the whole Edward Scissorhands reenactment on my carpeted stairs.

And, not least of all, I wish my son would have faith that the sky isn't going to fall, chocolate won't be declared an illegal substance, and his musical future is *not* ruined, just because he hit the wrong piano keys in a moment of madness.

Truth be told, our kids might never *get it*. Not in the way we hope, anyway. Their brains are just wired differently. Not in a loose connection, sparks-flying-out-the-sockets kind of way, but more like an avant-garde art installation that only makes sense if you squint, tilt your head, and accept that logic has almost certainly left the building.

And that's okay. Because they're not broken, they're not missing parts. They're just following a blueprint we've never seen before - one that doesn't come with instructions, translations, or a helpline that accepts chicken nuggets as valid currency.

The following show is brought to you by an anxiety-riddled Mum who lost her last bag of nerves at a dentist appointment today... that she didn't even make it into! Nope – I broke down at the *door*, and gave a hard pass on the chair.

I'm fairly certain I both offended and confused the poor dental squad, who were fully prepped to jab my gums with pointy things and chip away at my enamel. But alas, dear sirs, today was *not* your day. Your instruments may be sterile, but my soul was not.

Since then, I've cried hysterically, gifted myself a headache, and, because I'm clearly thriving, decided to stay up past midnight to plough my Ministry of Worry onto paper. Well... laptop, but the sentiment still stands.

Why is it, as full-grown adults allegedly equipped with logic, we spiral over things our bodies *need*? Essential care, basic survival, etc. And yet, for our babies, we'll suburban-gladiator style mine sweep the area, in armour made of slippers and an oversized Oddie, with determination over fear, purpose over reasoning.

And more waffle than Broad Street Diner in New Jersey!

✦✦✦ Incoming Call to the Neurodiverse Parent Helpline ✦✦✦

Hotline: *"Hello, you've reached the neurodiverse hotline. You grow 'em, we know 'em. And together, we'll dodge flying shoes, wild moods, and crayons in your espresso foam. What fresh chaos can we assist with today?"*

Parent: *"Yes, hi. I'm in dire need of clarification. And maybe redemption? Two days ago, this particular blue t-shirt was the holy grail of wardrobe choices. Now, after being lovingly laundered and returned to my son's drawer, he won't even look at it, and screamed at me when I went to pull it out. What gives?"*

Hotline*: "OK! When you say 'wash', do you mean you fumigated the fabric, drowned the dirt, and gave it a good old rub-a-dub-dub in the machine with other clothes?"*

Parent: *"Yes. That's what I did. Why?""*

Hotline: *"I think I've found your problem in the system.*
You have indirectly destroyed the emotional attachment your child had with that t shirt. Congratulations.
You may as well cut your losses and throw out the offending garment.
But be aware - the second you do, those sunshine-made memories will come back, and your child will spend four to six hours crying at you for discarding the cottonware."

Parent: "*Great. Just great. Anything else I should know?"*

Hotline: *"Just this: the green plate you spent three weeks searching for, and paid an obscene amount of money to get?*
That will also betray you in the near future.
Brace accordingly as you're pretty much screwed!
Now you have a nice day!"

✦✦✦ End Call ✦✦✦

Oh, wouldn't that be helpful? I mean, in a somewhat soul-destroying, mind-frying, awareness-wondering, emotionally-draining, logic-defying, sock-launching, sanity-splintering kind of way … but still!

Actually, I'm going to pass. I don't think my coffee is strong enough for that kind of chastisement! It's bad enough when my daughter, now 5ft6, sits scrolling through shoes online with me, spots a pair of trainers with a solid inch of wedge going on, and says, without a moment's grace,

"You should get them. Then you'd be a normal-height person!"

Ouch! If she weren't my kid, I'd have laughed it off, maybe. But instead, I gave her that sideways glance of horror, took a long, theatrical breath, and threatened to knock her into next week for her cheek. She knew I was joking, of course. But when I asked her if she actually *heard* the words fall from her mouth, like a thunder of hippos, leaping free from the top of a waterfall, she nodded solemnly, eyes wide, and said,

"Oh yes, I heard them.
But it was too late.
They'd already jumped."

And then she continued to laugh so loud and unapologetically. The kind that turns heads and makes people question if you've lost your marbles or found new ones.

That laughter, seasoned with a pinch of horror and a heap of ridiculousness, is *exactly* why I encourage that kind of nonsense. Because, as cliche as it is, *laughter really is the best medicine.* And for a child who wrestles daily with anxiety, who overthinks and underestimates herself, it's a tonic she deserves in unlimited doses.

And, truthfully? It helps me too.

I honestly believe that being a Mum has brought out the best in me, but also the worst. It's shown me what real love is - deep, messy, unconditional love, but in doing so, highlighted how little of it I truly knew before. It's given me purpose, and filled me up with a sense of worth I didn't know I was missing. But in turn, it's unearthed so much loneliness and spoon-fed self-doubt from my younger years.

Sometimes I wonder if I came flat-packed with emotional damage. Like, someone skipped step three, forgot to install the inner peace, and left me with an extra screw I now carry around in the form of social anxiety.

Allen keys and broken dreams, that's what I'm made of... *Well, that, along with caffeine, body ink, and sarcasm.*

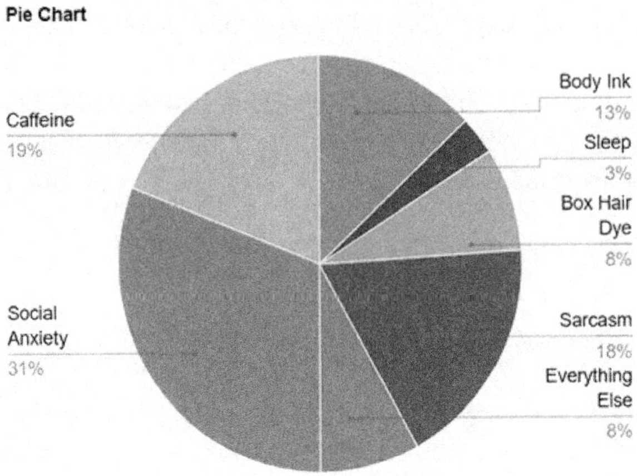

Did that moment really need a pie chart to highlight my ineptitude?

Absolutely not, *especially* now that it's been reduced to a lifeless array of greys, thanks to the criminal cost of printing in colour. What was once a joyful, rainbow-filled explosion of chaos and yet clarity, now looks like a depressed unicorn trying to express itself using only office printer toner.

But since my mind went off on an *'Ooo shiny'* spiral, down the path of *'How easy is it to make a pie chart?'* and into the depths of *'Tomorrow my house will be a shrine of laminated pie charts ranking the kids' chores and general readiness to do better'*...

Well, here we are!

Sleep, as you can tell, barely makes the cut, while box hair dye sits proudly up top, right next to sarcasm... because those are the true essentials of life. The things that keep me sweet, like popcorn on an oil-drum-made BBQ in Iraq! Totally unregulated, mildly dangerous, and somehow still the highlight of the day.

And with that, I shall end this chapter with one more neurodiverse helpline episode, because, well, why not?

You're welcome.

✦✦✦ Incoming Call to the Neurodiverse Child Helpline ✦✦✦

Hotline: *"Hello, you've reached the Neurodiverse Child Support Line, where we translate adult frills, track the late juice refills, and provide emergency backup for when you just can't sit still. What seems to be the crisis?"*

Child: *"Yes, hi. My mum RUINED my blue t-shirt. It used to smell like sunshine and Oreos. Now it smells like... a burden. And complete sadness."*

Hotline: *"Oh no. That's a Code 42: Fabric Betrayal. Did she wash it?"*

Child: *"YES! With the OTHER clothes. Like it's just... a shirt. Not my special one that makes me jump higher and helps me play piano better!"*

Hotline: "*I'm so sorry! Listen, we're going to log this under 'Parental Emotional Homicide - Cotton Edition.' Now, I have to ask. Have you cried yet?"*

Child: *"Not yet. I was planning a meltdown for around dinnertime."*

Hotline: *"Perfect. We recommend you insist on spaghetti, the one you've always understandably refused to eat, for maximum sauce-slinging impact. And don't forget to shout something abstract mid-cry. Maybe 'My elbows feel betrayed!' or 'YOU NEVER ASKED THE T-SHIRT HOW IT FELT!' That always hits hard."*

Child: *"Got it. Anything else?"*

Hotline: *"Just this: when your Mum tries to say "It's only a t-shirt", look her dead in the eye and whisper, "And it was only your wedding dress." That'll do the trick."*

Child: "*Ok, thank you. You guys are the best.*"

Hotline: *"We know. Now go forth, young warrior. And may your cereal be forever crunchy, never soggy!"*

✦✦✦ End Call ✦✦✦

Notes From the Edge

10th March 2025 ♡

Kitty cuddles make everything better!

It's day four of the new diet. Day four of the misery... The hunger... The internal disappointment when my calorie count only allows for one biscuit... And honestly, it sucks more than a swarm of mosquitoes at the Rio Carnival.

Yes, I promised myself over a week ago that I'd hit the road running this time... except I got rid of the treadmill last month in favour of a boxercise machine, so I guess that means I should be hitting the lights, punching? Honestly, I don't know. ⋆˚｡ But what I do know is that four days into this so-called health-kick, I am seriously regretting my life choices.

Like a pigeon who's crash-landed in a crazy lady's garden and is now being forced to live as her long-lost parakeet. Not so much the choice to drop a few pounds, but more so, the ones that led up to me needing to drop said pounds.

You see, back in my 20s and early 30s, I ate whatever I wanted. And with it, laughed in the face of fat pants, like they were a bedtime story designed to scare carb-lovers into submission.

But now, in my 40s? Yeah, those fat pants are holding my life together like a loyal best friend. The kind who forgives your questionable decisions, never judges your third slice of cake, and gently reassures you that somehow, together, you'll get through this 🧑‍🤝‍🧑

Anyway, today I felt like a hero, walking around the shop for fresh green vegetables... And an end-of-life doula by the time I got home, knowing full well those green beans and broccoli stems will likely rot at the bottom of my fridge.

If you can't tell already from the sheer joy I'm smothering across the page, my coffee intake is down to three measly mugs a day. I could have more if I drank it black – zero calories in black coffee. But there's also zero pleasure, zero purpose, and zero reason to live ⎯⩘⩘♡

Melodramatic much?
Yeah, maybe.
I blame the lack of go-go juice.

In other, less depressing news, the infamous Mr. D is back on the keys. The lesson was a hit, his viola playing skills, a surprise. And the promise that next week, we'll start something new, a result in my son's eyes.

I am honestly in awe of my boy's 'pick up and carry on' attitude. Though we've missed three weeks, what with holidays and illness, my Elton Junior slid back onto that piano stool like a pro ♪𝄞₊˚⊹ He sat and played with so much feeling, and understanding for the story behind the notes. And at the end, took the compliments in his stride...

Before firing yet more bewildering questions at Mr. D.

That kid never misses a beat, or, an opportunity to completely baffle his teacher with debates that, I'm fairly certain, have never been voiced in the history of music!

I love how his mind works, how it springboards from one topic to something vaguely related in five seconds or less. I love his passion, his hopes, and his dreams to one day perform on stage with Mr. D, his music hero ★

But the emotional pendulum has since swung. And his mood? Depleted. Like a lone, soggy French fry at the bottom of a takeout bag. Though once golden and full of promise, it's now limp, cold, and deeply disappointing... Urgh! Food analogies are a bad idea today, especially the junk food ones!

I think, however, it was the light-up drawing board that really knocked him down. It didn't want to stay 'lit up', because, well, he'd neglected to tell me that it needed charging. And just like that, tracing geometric shapes became nothing more than a distant dream.

He couldn't re-roll his mat after yoga either. It didn't like him, apparently. The blue spongy inanimate object that previously lay so quietly was now causing shrieks of distress. And so, it was soon thrust into my arms, like a crying baby who needed its Mama to reattach the elastic bands of togetherness.

So much for yoga being a calm and happy activity ॐ

I guess we can't always be in a good place. I, for one, am struggling today. Not just because of the diet (although, let's be honest, depriving myself of snacks is hardly lifting my spirits).

But more than that, I'm doubting my right to be here. To write this book. To believe in myself enough to see it through...

I have so desperately wanted this. To put my words out there. To publish something real and raw, something that's mine. And if you're reading this, then I guess I fought through the noise that tells me I can't...That I'm an idiot for trying... That I'm wasting my time, because who the heck would take me seriously?

⌈✦ CHoO CHoO, ALL ABOARD the train of mild personal sabotage and panic-powered ambition. With imposter syndrome at the wheel, anxiety laying the tracks, and a buffet cart serving nothing but regret and cling film-wrapped chaos and cold egg sandwiches, you'd be crazy not to jump aboard! ✦⌋

╰----➤

I suppose when you've spent long enough wading through criticism, second-guessing everything you are, it leaves a mark. Believing in yourself starts to feel like wishful thinking dressed as a motivational meme.

And, as I've said before, probably somewhere in this book, possibly while ranting about the educational system or a poorly designed workbook, I *never* want my kids to feel like that. I don't want them carrying doubts that were never theirs to begin with. I don't want them to think they have to earn love or audition for acceptance.

And they won't. Not while I'm here, for I shall raise those babies up so high that they can no longer see the negativity in the world. That they will know, without question, they are worthy, they are loved, they are enough.

Because that's how it should be.

And maybe some of that will come from telling this story. Not just mine, but ours, my emotionally charged ostrich and me ♡♡

A story of learning and unlearning. Of breaking cycles and building something better. And of course, that of all the people, not least of all my beautiful, almost teenage daughter, who unwittingly got dragged into it, along the way,

> "Some days are just bad days, that's all. You have to experience sadness to know happiness, and I remind myself that not every day is going to be a good day, that's just the way it is!" – Dita Von Teese

Chapter 17: Harbouring Chaos

Because when you're the safe place for everyone else, there's not always room to fall apart.

Do you ever get one of those nights, where the pillow just isn't comfy? It doesn't matter what you do, no matter how much you twist it, flap it, hit it, punch it, or verbally abuse it... It's just not comfy. It's not doing it for you.

And suddenly you're threatening divorce… from the pillow.

That's me on a far too regular occurrence. I find myself sitting bolt upright at gone 3am, and aggressively launching my pillow across the room, like it'd personally betrayed me and all my ancestors. And then, hindsight, as well as the need to retrieve the apparent pincushion, kicks in.

Did the pillow *actually* do anything wrong? No.
Was I completely rational in that moment? Also no.

But that's the thing. I wasn't just angry at the pillow. The pillow was the final straw. The last push. The quietest trigger in a brain that's already fizzing with everything it hadn't finished, fixed, washed, replied to, or emotionally processed. And this, I've come to realise, is what adult emotional dysregulation looks like.

Unlike my child, it's not always dramatic. It's not always obvious. Sometimes, it's whisper-screaming into my IKEA bedding because life feels like a community project, for which I'm the only person making any real effort. Other times, it's the coffee, tea, and sugar pots being stacked in the wrong order. Again.

And yes, I know it's ridiculous. I know it's small. But in that moment, it's not really about the jars. It's about the principle. It's about being ignored. It's about asking for one simple thing, one tiny, ritualistic comfort, and still being denied.

Standing on the brink of a full caddy-based breakdown, I cry out:
"Why? Why can't they just go back in the right order? I've had them like this for over twenty years. At least four of you lot have been mentally equipped to understand the system for. And yet still, the emotional demands are not being met!"

And just like that, the thread snaps.
The jars are wrong.
The universe is wrong.
And my much-needed coffee is now poisoned by disarray and frustration.

Of course, my theatrical display, complete with arm waving and a semi-serious tone, leads the daughter, aka the most likely mis-stacking suspect, to fall about laughing. And my pain, my *actual mental pain*, swirls around the bottom of the now semi-warm cuppa.

That's how I cope. That's how I claw my way through coffee-stained chaos and find meaning in the madness, even if it takes me all the way to California...

A wee tribute to my biological dad there, whose ashes were laid to rest in Dana Point, a coastal town just off California.

He hadn't seen me since I was a baby, and I don't have a single memory of him. But whenever I'm standing on a beach, looking out at the sea, I feel something. A pull. A quiet kind of connection that I can't quite explain. There's something in the rhythm of the waves, in the endless rise and fall, that makes it feel like he's closer. Like maybe he's seen the chaos I'm wading through, and he's out there somewhere, cheering me on from a place just out of reach.

I don't know what kind of father he would have been. Maybe useless. Maybe worse than useless. But I like to think, wherever he ended up, he'd be proud of the kind of mum I've become.

Yes, I spiral. Often. Over jars, socks, cold toast, loud chewing, and the feeling of cool air being too *air-y* on the skin.

And humour is my release valve. It's either laugh or cry. And frankly, crying messes with my mascara, which I just don't have the emotional budget for!

It's not that I hide behind the exaggerated drama. It's not a mask or some carefully curated image I prefer people see. It's just a response, a switch that flicks, kickstarting an almost Tourettes-style outburst. And weirdly, I've come to love it… Although not so much when it gets me in trouble!

Funny story - I'm unofficially-officially banned from at least one high street optician chain, three MOT stations, a dental practice, a pet store, a car sales forecourt, and one NHS service team. Possibly two. But they stopped answering my emails, so the jury's still out.

I ramble a shamble quite freely. And what should be a calm discussion over a minor problem, inconvenience, mistake, etc, quickly turns into a showdown of unwanted truths dressed up in titillating tassels and tutus.

As a one-time-only burlesque model, a gig for giggles, I do indeed realise the impact such items can have. But I should make clear – my previous statement was simply a metaphor for the pitched battle I, on occasion, find myself in.

That being said, a cheeky swoosh of a tassel might resolve some of these problematic situations. Or, failing that, at least make my permanent record far more interesting.... No, actually. Let's not do that.

I have this habit, this very real, well-practised habit, of saying *"I'm fine"* when I'm absolutely, categorically *not fine*. I say it with a smile, sometimes a little laugh, like I'm auditioning for the role of some low-budget fan-only movie. And most of the time, people believe me.

Because to be fair, I *do* look fine… right up until I don't. Right up until I'm aggressively organising the kitchen utensils drawer while muttering about injustice and system failure like a woman possessed. Or, say, delivering a two-hour theatrical monologue to an imaginary NHS board. All because a sonographer tried to carry out an ultrasound scan for my daughter's dodgy heart valve on his own. Despite her being twelve. Anxious. And visibly uncomfortable.

This wasn't just a rant. It was a *performance*. There were waving arms. There was pacing. There may have been a Facebook video that outlined his,

"...utter contempt for me and my wildly inconvenient request that my daughter be treated with basic respect and human dignity. And then, to my horror, he suggested that, if his solo scanning approach didn't suit,

my son, eight years old with Disability tags hanging round his neck, should sit alone in the destitute corridor, like a beggar in the streets of Delhi. He'd have been a flight risk within minutes, thanks to the open doors, no supervision, and only panicked cries echoing in his heart as he desperately searched for me in the labyrinth of bleak NHS corridors…"

You can probably see where I started to lose hope. And dignity. And a grip on reality.

I even attempted to call the complaints department. But luckily, for the *Patron Saint of Solo-Sonology,* they were closed as it was a weekend. Had they answered, I might've gone into a full Shakespearean meltdown. And that wouldn't have gone well for any of us.

I'm pretty sure this uncontrollable urge to blurt out sarcastic monologues at full volume in wildly inappropriate settings is some kind of fight-or-flight response, coated in ADHD, caffeine, and an unhealthy dose of Mama Bear protective instinct.

Since having kids, my sarcastic throwbacks have absolutely escalated. My nonsense filter? Completely clogged. Like the Hoover, I always forget to empty. And the urge to burn metaphorical bridges? Especially when some moron, fluent in *"I'm going to press all your buttons, starting with number seven"*, is standing right on them? That's reached new heights.

I mean, I'm not into arson, but the phrase *"Don't burn your bridges"*? Please. I'm already toasting marshmallows and rating the fire out of ten.

Is this a normal response to parenting? Probably not. Definitely not if you're going by books with titles like '*Elevating the Child: A Mindful Journey to Behavioural Refinement*'... Don't worry, I just made that one up!

But my kids, my bin lids, my tweedles dees and giant fleas - they get me. Back in the first chapter, *Survival*, I talked about this. About how my son saw me, I mean *really* saw me, in a way no one else ever had. Not my mum. Not siblings, friends, partners, anyone.

But both my daughter and my son do. They *see* me. All of me. The mess, the mood swings, the once delicate and now smudged eyeliner. The nervous energy that comes out sideways as sarcasm. And somehow, they still run into my arms like I'm the actual Easter Bunny! They laugh with me. At me. Sometimes both at the same time.

And they do it freely, without fear or worry, because they know that even when the rest of the world feels too loud, too fast, too confusing, I am their safe place. They come to me with those tangled thoughts, big feelings, and half-finished sentences. And they trust I'll help them unpick it all, even when I can't fix it.

Cue the mum who stays up until 4am trying to solve said problem, while simultaneously hating the world for gifting me an obnoxious amount of stress and frustration... when all I *really* want to do is eat cake and sleep. Only eating cake completely voids the thirty-four lettuce leaves I heroically consumed earlier. So now I'm tired *and* nutritionally confused.

Funny moment going on right now with my son, as I'm sat on the sofa trying to edit this chapter on my phone...

Me: "What was wrong with your chicken last night?"
Him: "Nothing. Well, there was... but I can't explain it."
Me: "Come on, I need to know so I can fix it for next time."
Him: "There was nothing wrong. Well, there *was*, but I *can't* explain it."

This looped another three or four times before I bellowed, in full courtroom mode, "*Tell me what's wrong with the chicken?!*" to which he calmly replied, "I. Don't. Know." before bursting out laughing at my fake-stern face.

This naturally led into a tickle-fest, which he's still terrible at. Still very much in the stabby-fingers stage. And as he escaped (or was graciously released from) my grip, he sang out *"Halle-monia!"* on repeat, giggling in that proper, from-the-belly, injections kind of way.

I still have no idea what *"Halle-monia!"* means, or what was wrong with the chicken. I'll try making it again in four to seven days and see if the issue has resolved itself, or if I need to find yet another new brand.

Is this how every mum feels? Constantly overthinking, emotionally spiralling, and planning for at least nine possible disasters, all before breakfast?

I'd say dads too, but judging from personal encounters, they tend to lean more towards *'go with the flow'* and *'it'll work itself out'*, which, honestly, is probably one of the few reasons I'd volunteer for one of those swap-bodies-for-24-hours scenarios.

Well... that and the whole helicopter thing. Obviously!

Actually, I think what I'd really want from a body-swap situation isn't the whole *'understand the opposite sex'* thing. It's just the luxury of not having to do my eyebrows before leaving the house!

Like, I imagine waking up, rolling out of bed, pulling on whatever's closest to the radiator, and just... going outside. Without checking my reflection, without dabbing concealer on my under-eye bags and painting on the contour. Without balancing the now *very obvious* silver streaks with equal amounts of desperation on either side of my parting.

I'd love to walk into Tesco and be celebrated for showing up at all. To look less like a hobo and more like a hero… just for buying milk.

✦✦✦

"Attention all shoppers! Can we get a round of applause for the magnificent woman in aisle three. Yes, the one in yesterday's hoodie and questionable hair, who has bravely shown up to buy milk despite looking like she's just returned from a gap year in a house full of unsupervised children and unresolved trauma.
Ma'am, you are the glue holding this society together."

✦✦✦

And before anyone starts, I get that not all women feel this pressure. And not all men are immune to it. I once knew a guy who wore winged eyeliner so crisp that it looked like my granny had ironed it, along with my grandpa's hankies and a fresh load of bed linen.

But still.

I've developed this… I don't know. Pressure? Expectation? Some kind of built-in fear, maybe, that we, the children and I, need to present. To be more than just tidy. To look *'put together'* for the outside world, even when I feel like a bin on fire.

That if I don't, society will look even further down its wart-covered nose at us. That I shall be labelled useless. And my children? Declared homeless, flea-infested, illiterate biscuit junkies with no table manners and questionable reading skills. All because I left the house without a to-go packet of baby wipes, and forgot to brush someone's hair.

And to some degree, I feel like it's the same performance everywhere. A *'make it look good, even when the wheels are coming off'* show, which is why I wasn't 100% sure I wanted to include this chapter. I mean, it's kind of off-topic. Kind of off-vibe. Not really part of the grand plan, assuming you can call the scribbles my son and I made on the office floor last year a *'plan'* at all.

But the more the book unravelled *(a bit like my knitting project, which now lives half done in a box under the bed)*, the more it became obvious: this chapter matters. Because this isn't just about understanding neurodivergence, or parenting, or meltdowns in supermarket aisles.

No, it's about *unity*. It's about having someone, even if it's just me, say *"Yeah, same"* so you don't feel like you're losing your mind in the dark, alone, while everyone else is pretending they've got it together… The keyword there being *pretending*. Because let's be honest, most of us are just one biscuit free-falling into our coffee, away from a full emotional breakdown.

So if something I write makes you feel seen, properly, honestly, not alone, then that's reason enough for me to keep writing, to publish, to lay my soul bare… like a sad rotisserie chicken at 8pm in ASDA. A bit overcooked, slightly unravelled, but still here. Still warm. Still trying.

"So Ms Jones, why do you feel you need therapy?" That's what my future therapist is going to say. And I shall hold up this and the next three books I write, bow my head, and reply,

"Because I overshared. Publicly. Repeatedly. And in doing so, realised that I have *so many* feelings, and no suitable boxes to put them in."

She'll nod, make a note, and then I'll likely launch into a long and entirely unnecessary story about how I once cried because the cats scrambled over my desk and tore a page in my brand-new diary. A diary that had been in my life for exactly four days and had become a symbol of me finally getting it together.

I'll explain that I name household appliances out loud like it's normal, such as

Mindy the Mixer. That I once tried to emotionally bond with a pair of hair straighteners because they were helping me through a particularly traumatic hair-don't situation. And that I am now the proud owner of pipe cutters, having thrown on my ill-fitted 'Can Do' hat and replumbed the kitchen sink with zero know-how or landlord consent.

I'll tell her about the time I had a full-blown internal crisis because someone parked slightly over the white line in a car park and ruined what could've been a beautiful parallel parking moment. She'll try not to pull a face as I explain how I considered leaving a note, then imagined them finding the note, feeling ashamed, spiralling, and self-sabotaging their entire life... all before deciding it was probably fine and going home to eat half a tub of homemade cookies instead.

She'll pause, smile too kindly, and ask, "And how do you typically manage your emotions?"

To which I'll answer, "Mostly with a coffee binge, a nervous laugh, and a 45-minute verbal spiral where I pretend I'm fine but accidentally confess to six different emotional crises and a mild identity shift."

I can see it coming. And then some!

Am I the crazy woman who recently carried her nearly-nine-year-old son around the supermarket when he needed to get away from the world, only to be scowled at by some mothball-infused grunter, like he was an infectious disease? Yes.

Am I also the person who loudly externalises her road rage with outbursts of, *"I see the only signal you're capable of giving is the one that proves you're a complete and utter moron who shouldn't have a driving licence. Or a cat. I feel you'd be mean to cats. No cats for you"*? Also yes.

And I guess that's part of why you've kept reading this book.

And why you might be *mildly intrigued* about the next one. You know, the one I casually slipped into conversation with my imaginary therapist a page or two back?

Just checking you're still paying attention! I'm a million roads away from getting this bad boy on the shelves. Or on your bedside table, next to the water bottle you swore you'd start drinking from, and the tag from that jumper you ripped off in a mad morning rush. *(For the record, I'm currently harbouring at least four empty cups and bottles between the bedroom and my office in the next room. I don't even know how. Or why. It just... happens!)*

And honestly, that probably sums up most of this chapter. Things piling up, emotions spilling over, and me trying to make sense of it all between mouthfuls of cold coffee and half-formed thoughts.

I don't have a tidy message to leave you with here. No inspirational quote, no parenting revelation, no magical fix for emotional overload.

Just this: If you're muddling through, rage-whispering at your predictive text for putting *'duck'* when you definitely didn't mean *'duck'*... If you're crumbling over the extra seven plates your kids managed to use for no logical reason whatsoever... Or if you've threatened to turn the WIFI off until the end of time, because the dirty sock is still rotting on the stairs... Same.

> *You're doing better than you think. And if no one's told you that lately, let this be it.*

However, if none of that applies to you, if this chapter gave you nothing more than a laugh, a moment of *"Geoff from HR would definitely file this under wildly inappropriate but weirdly relatable,"* and a chance to forget your to-do list for five minutes, then honestly, that's a win too.

Because sometimes, all we really need is to feel a little lighter. To snort-laugh over shared chaos. And if that's what this gave you? Well then… that's just a Brucey Bonus.

Now go finish that cup of tea you forgot about an hour ago.

Or don't. No judgment here!

The Outro

Feathers ruffled.
Mission mostly accomplished.

So, here we are. At the end.
Or at least, my end of this story.

If you've made it this far, thank you. Whether you read this book in one coffee-fuelled sitting, or picked it up and put it down a hundred times between meltdowns, meetings, or moments of self-doubt, you stayed. And that means more than I can say.

As you can probably tell, I wasn't aiming for wisdom, but rather honesty *(albeit with a few dodgy metaphors thrown in!)* It was never meant to be a guidebook. Or a *how-to fix-it* manual.

But rather a story. A messy, ridiculous, beautiful story. Mine, yes. But maybe a little bit of yours, too.

Because parenting, especially parenting a child who experiences the world differently, isn't a straight path. It's winding. Wild. Often isolating. A chaotic storm of a journey that is both soul-awakening and soul-wrecking in equal measures.

And yet, somehow, within the overwhelm and exhaustion, come those moments of breathtaking clarity. Of fierce love. Of joy that feels even sweeter because you fought so hard for it.

That moment your child says something completely unexpected… and you realise that they not only listened, but they understood. That day, a meltdown softened instead of exploding, and the relief felt like this huge adrenaline rush.

That ridiculous healing laughter, on that one day when you needed it most. That one person who got it, without any kind of judgment.

It's all there. And this book?

- ★ It's for anyone who's ever felt like they're parenting in the dark.
- ★ For the families still at the beginning, Googling diagnoses and wondering if they're strong enough, which, for the record, you are.
- ★ For the ones deep in the trenches, navigating school battles and sensory overload. And the ache of being misunderstood.
- ★ For the parents years in, who still need reminding that you're doing OK. More than OK.
- ★ And for those who aren't parenting at all, but came here out of love or curiosity or kindness. To you, thank you for listening. Thank you for caring. And for not treating us like an inconvenience or a punchline.

Because this journey? It's not about having all the answers. It's not a tick-box exercise. Or a final exam. Instead, it's about showing up, tired, imperfect, and still trying. And believing, deep down, that that alone is enough.

I'm still learning. Still unlearning. Still getting it wrong. But I do know this:

Love matters more than perfection.
Connection matters more than control.
And laughter, even the exhausted kind,
is its own kind of survival.

If this book has offered you anything, comfort, clarity, a bit of sarcasm-fuelled solidarity, I'm glad. Because *that* was the point, from the very beginning.

Not to hand out *wisdom* like free samples at a supermarket, but to say: yep, it's a mess, and nope, you're not the only one wading through it.

We made it.
You, me, and whatever half-drunk cup of coffee got us through.

And that? And that counts for a lot.

An Open Letter

I wasn't going to write this bit. I figured I'd said enough, probably more than enough, if we're being honest. Some of you may have even wondered when I was going to stop rambling on.

But as I reached the end, I kept getting this nagging feeling.
Like I'd skimmed past something that still needed saying.

And then I realised, even though I've already talked about our diagnosis story in bits and pieces, I need to circle back one last time. Because that's where the stuff I still struggle with lives. Where the guilt lingers, even now.

Not from the shock. Not even from the strange sense of relief I found from 'knowing'. But from when we were deep in the assessment process, and I was joining every online group I could find, just to try and make sense of the world we'd been thrown into.

For the most part, I was a silent observer, soaking up other people's stories, comparing them to our own, trying to find where we fit, etc, etc. At that stage, we were entirely caught up in Autism, trying to navigate that world, figuring out what it meant for my son, for us, for everything. It felt huge enough on its own, like more than enough to handle.

And, I'm slightly ashamed to admit it now, but more than once I caught myself thinking, *"I'm glad that's not us! All those parents battling both Autism and ADHD? That sounds like an actual nightmare!"*

I'm so sorry for that thought. I wasn't judging anyone. I was just scared and overwhelmed by it all.

I couldn't see past the day in front of me, let alone imagine handling more. I just didn't have the emotional bandwidth or the understanding to stretch beyond what we were already holding...

But then came our final CAMHS meeting, the big day, the *'signing off.'* And just as I thought we might be nearing the finish line, the paediatrician looked at me and said gently, *"It would be a good idea to follow this up with an ADHD assessment."*

And just like that, my world shattered. Not because I didn't love him enough. Not because I wasn't willing. But because I was tired, terrified, and clinging to the idea that maybe we were done with the whole diagnosis journey. It had already been so long, and I didn't want more paperwork. I didn't want more unknowns. And I definitely didn't want the weight of the ADHD stigma.

Because that, in my mind, was something else.

I knew Autism. We'd lived in that space for a while. And though it took time, months and even years, to reach that understanding, it had become familiar. Not easy, but known. I'd read the books. I'd joined the groups. I'd even found language for what once felt unexplainable.

I'd cried, grieved, adjusted, and eventually found a strange kind of peace with it.

But ADHD? That felt different. Louder. Wilder. Harder. It came with a set of mental scars I didn't even know I was carrying. And looking back, I know exactly where those scars came from.

See, I grew up in the '80s and '90s, when ADHD wasn't explained with compassion. It was whispered about. It meant *naughty*. It meant *out of control*. It meant *that kid*. And I knew *that* kid because she was my little sister.

I remember the chaos. The waiting rooms where she bounced in her seat, ran in circles, talked too fast, too loud, too much. I remember the looks from strangers. The disapproving sighs. The way other parents shielded their children, as if hyperactivity were contagious.

And I remember my mum doing her best, which, to be honest, isn't something I say often.

I can still hear her voice, *"She's got ADHD"*, like it was a warning, a reason to excuse the things they were already judging. Because back then, there was no talk of executive function, dopamine-seeking, or emotional regulation. There was just blame. And shame. And kids being treated like problems, with parents made to feel like failures.

That's the story that had wrapped around my thoughts, like a rope, tied tightly. And when I read posts from other parents, parents whose children had both Autism and ADHD, I winced. I judged. And I said, *"Yeah, I couldn't deal with that!"*

So to every single one of you walking that rocky path... I'm sorry. Not for your journey. Not for your brilliant, vibrant children. But for the way I saw you. I'm sorry for the story I'd been telling myself – a story built from stigma, not truth. A story that was never mine to tell. And certainly never fair to believe.

Being completely honest, learning to do better hasn't been a clean, neat process. It's been messy. It's been humbling. It's involved staring directly into the parts of myself I don't like. But it's also been healing for me, for my family, and for the tired, confused parent I used to be.

I now understand that ADHD isn't a problem. It's not a tantrum in a waiting room. It's not a child who *can't behave*. It's not bad parenting. It's not failure.

It's just a different kind of brain. A different rhythm. A different way of seeing the world, full of motion, magic, and potential.

Yes, sometimes it is hard. But sometimes... It's extraordinary. And that deserves to be recognised with honesty. With love. With dignity. And so much more.

It's strange, isn't it? How a single moment, a new diagnosis, a quiet sentence in a meeting, can completely rearrange your world. For me, that moment smashed something wide open. Not just in fear for what lay ahead, but in a realisation I wasn't expecting.

Because as I read more, joined more groups, and listened more closely, not just to others, but to myself, I started to recognise the familiar traits.

The scattered focus and all-consuming passions.
The disorganisation and forgotten appointments.
The huge feelings and racing thoughts.
The ache of isolation, paired with the struggle to be around others.
The brilliant ideas that never made it out of the starting blocks...

I wasn't just seeing *my son.* I was finally seeing *me* – the version of me I never had the language for. And suddenly, that double diagnosis didn't feel like a punishment anymore.

It felt like a key.
An open doorway.
A map I never knew I needed.

Through understanding him, I began to understand myself. And with that understanding came something else I hadn't expected...

Compassion.

For my sister. For my mother. For the parents in those chaotic waiting rooms. For the children being judged when they were simply being themselves. And for the younger version of me, too – the one who didn't know what she was seeing, but felt it anyway.

Because if, like me, you're raising a child with Autism, ADHD, both, or something else entirely, that means living in the deep end, every single moment.

These kids? They are fierce. They are bright. They are complex. And they are deeply, deeply loved, even on the difficult days. The impossible ones. The hiding-in-the-bathroom-with-a-leftover-bagel-just-to-feel-like-a-human-being-for-five-minutes days.

So when someone turns to you and says, "I couldn't do what you're doing," try to hear what might really be behind it. Yes, sometimes their words are clumsy, wrapped in discomfort, awkwardness, or a lack of understanding. But often, underneath all that, there's awe. A quiet kind of respect. The kind that sees your strength, even when you've forgotten it's there.

Please, don't take it as a dig. Don't let it trick you into thinking you don't belong in the same room as everyone else. Because more often than not, what they're really saying is, "I see you carrying something heavy, and I honestly don't know how you do it."

And no, accepting that doesn't mean you're validating anyone's misconceptions. But rather, you're redefining what strength looks like. You're showing the world what love looks like in motion. You're showing up, facing chaos, and still finding moments of joy, humour, and heart.

There's beauty in that. There's power in that. And you don't have to downplay any of it.

So, to every parent walking this road, thank you.

Thank you for helping me unlearn what I thought I knew. For holding space for a story I hadn't lived yet.

I'm still trying to figure things out. But I'm with you, fully, fiercely. And in messy, honest solidarity.

Much love and good vibes from us.